For

My Parents:

Lawrence and Rosemary Walcott

I am a better person because of their love, guidance and support.

For

My son and my daughter: Dominic and Dominique James,

The angels whom God has entrusted to my care

For

Victory World Church

The community in which I found my fullness of joy and rest in

Him

Acknowledgement

This book is dedicated to the following people for their love, encouragement, and support.

Dennis Griffith Ed.D ~ Professor and Mentor

Lois Sanders ~ Mentor and Friend

Valerie Hunter ~ Friend and Accountability Partner

Troy and Torey Banks ~ Friends and Exhorters

Table of Content

Foreword..11

Preface..13

Chapter One: The Awesomeness of God

God's Countenance...16

How Great is Our God...21

Levels of Nourishment..24

Prayer Works..29

Simplicity..33

They Do Exist...36

Washed Clean...40

Wonderfully and Fearfully Made......................................44

Chapter Two: Praise

Forgiven..50

I Love You, Lord...52

Nature Praise...54

Today..56

Whooping it up for the Lord...58

Chapter Three: Counsel

All in His Name 63

Are You Ready 67

By What Measure 71

How Low Can You Go 74

Humble and Contrite 78

Of What Does Your Heart Speak 82

Running Towards Destruction 85

The Beauty of Betrayal 88

The Feeding of Spirits 92

Women of God 96

Chapter Four: Deliverance

About Face 100

Deliverance from Immorality 104

Fear Not 108

Guises of Enemy 112

In Him, This Too Shall Pass 117

Real Life Reality Game Show 120

Sanctified, Whole, and Blameless 123

Stubbornness or Obedience: Punishment or Reward 126

The Pinnacle of the Mountain 131

Under Attack..136
Warfare...140

Chapter Five: Relationship

A Most Valued Possession...143
And Then he Saved Me..147
As the Deer...149
At His Feet..153
But by the Grace of God..156
Comfort Food..160
Everlasting..163
In Whose Flock Are You Counted...............................164
Nothing Without Him...167
Reunited..171
Security under God's Protection...................................174
Speak, Lord...178
The Only One That Matters..182
Wait...185
Wisdom and Understanding..187

Chapter Six: The Promises of God

Believing in God's Provision……………………………………..192

Exceeding, Abundantly……………………………………...196

Rainbow……………………………………………………………..200

God's Promise of Fellowship……………………………...203

Priceless……………………………………………………………...206

Chapter Seven: Encouragement

Let Patience Have Her Perfect Way……………………………210

Merriment or Reverence: You Decide……………………....213

More Than A Conqueror………………………………………216

Spoken Words……………………………………………………..220

Wait for It…………………………………………………………..224

Chapter Eight: Brotherly Love

For Lisa………………………………………………………………228

Friendships in Christ……………………………………………..231

The Blessings of Brotherhood……………………………………235

To the Depths of Service……………………………………..238

Chapter Nine: Receiving, Releasing and Perpetuating the Blessing

Blessings Abound..242
Legacy...245
Smooth Transition of Leadership......................................250
Teachable Moments..253
This Little Light of Mine..256
Wrestling with a Purpose...259

Foreword

As a young girl, I always knew that I was going to write a book. The desire was as innate as breathing. Writing from the impressionable age of twelve, I penned every emotion; every disappointment; every blessing that came my way in the form of poetry. Although I wrote profusely, it had not dawned on me to keep a binder of my writings. As such, it was not until the age of sixteen that I started to compile my art. It was also at that age that I began to share and recite my work to those whom I loved and trusted.

As word of my writings got out and I matured in my thought process and skill; I was soon asked to write for and present at ticketed affairs. As this continued and although I was asked to, I never sold any of my work. It was my desire to wait until the opportune time to have my poetry bound and published throughout the world. It was my idea, or so I thought; that my work should be shared with the world as opposed to just a few.

With that in mind, I embarked on a journey of fluidity with my pen as I romanticized various experiences in my life. It was not until I found the Lord, and received the gift of the Holy Spirit that the anointing of writing was confirmed upon my life. Similarly, it was not until I found myself in His Word that I realized His purpose was that I used my experiences to draw others unto Him so that they too might be saved.

Accordingly, as surely as the Lord made His purpose known it became my pleasure to obey. As I committed myself to the task, He poured His word into my spirit tying memories of things I had since long forgotten.

A compilation of said experiences tied to the Word of God complete with Quick Trips around the Bible is what I have penned in obedience. Entitled, *The Writing's on the Wall: A Daily Devotional from the Heart of God, Season One* it is my heart that the spirit of the living God accompanies each and every copy and touches each and every person whose eyes seek to behold His word.

I pray God's peace, love, mercy, and favor on you all.
So That None Should Perish,
Danielle

Preface

As I lay in my bed the morning of Saturday, March 14, 2009 at 7:30. I felt the grieved heart of the Lord and heard His voice:

"Be watchful, be vigilant My people! For the adversary, like a snake, is tarrying about your ankles. Be mindful of Him, lest you be tempted and fall. Remember to keep my commandments at all times, walk in faith, and listen for My voice. When have I ever led you astray? I love you oh My children and I wish for none to perish. Turn ye from your wicked ways so My love can shine upon you once more! Secure yourself a place with me where you shall live forever. The world is fading, and shall not last, but I shall be forever."

"My wrath, though fleeting, will not be staved. The wicked will pay. The world will pass. But you, My children, if you will only turn back to Me you will be saved from this cup – the cup that shall come to pass."

"Turn back to Me, My children..." thus said the Lord.

It is with this Word in mind that I further seek to fulfill my purpose in Him by completing and publishing this book.

Please heed His voice.

Chapter One:

The Awesomeness of our God

In the light of the king's countenance is life; and his favor is as a cloud of the latter rain.

(Proverbs 16:15)

God's Countenance

Although my vocabulary is prolific, I had never heard or used the word countenance prior to my walk with Christ. Labeled by my friends as the *girl who spoke with her face*, I was familiar with the term, "Fix your face." However, not included in my purview; the word countenance was simply not a term used by my family members or by my friends. Accordingly so, I will never forget the first time the word was spoken to me.

I had entered the classroom of my colleague Naomi one morning to have our usual glory talk before the day got started. At that time, recently born again; I was spending an immense amount of time with God through daily readings, prayer and supplication, worship, praise, and inquiry. Through it all Naomi had become a catalyst in my relationship with God as well as someone to whom I could make myself accountable during my daily walk with Christ. As we shared our excitement about the ways of the Lord, she looked at me with a pleasant, though perplexing look. When asked what the matter was, she calmly responded; "Your countenance has changed!"

"What are you talking about?" I replied,

"Your face," she said. "The Holy Spirit rests upon you. I can see Him."

"Oh, that's weight;" I quipped. And as we continued our conversation, I never gave her comment another thought until a week and a half later when I was approached at the end of a Wednesday night Bible study by a church sister. As she moved within an arm's length of me, she cupped her hands on my face, and exclaimed, "Look at God!" Although I did not respond, I was instantaneously reminded of what Naomi had said a week and a half earlier – God's confirmation to the young in spirit.

Defined by the Cambridge Online Dictionary, countenance is *the appearance or expression of someone's face.* Synonymous with a look, or appearance; one's countenance expresses one's emotions. Found in context 52 times in both the Old and New Testaments of the Bible (KJV), countenance was used to describe looks of trepidation, guilt, fear, sorrow, love, praise, and trust in the Lord. Most importantly, however; countenance was also used to describe the glory of God.

Evidenced in Exodus 34:28-30,

> "And he was there with the LORD forty days and forty nights; he did neither eat bread, nor drink water. And he wrote upon the tablets the words of the covenant, the Ten Commandments. And it came to pass, when Moses came down from Mount Sinai with the two tablets of testimony in Moses' hand, when he came down from the mount that Moses knew not that the skin of his face shone while he talked with him." As a matter of fact, Moses' face shone so brightly with the glory of God that Aaron and the children of Israel were afraid to come close to him. (NASB)

To paraphrase, God's glory rested upon Moses' face after Moses spent forty days and nights of solace and communion with God.

What implication does this text have for us you might ask? Well, God's glory - His countenance – will rest upon us if we simply but spend time with Him. Is it any wonder that to build our relationship with Him both productive and reflective time must be invested? In Moses' instance, forty days and forty nights were spent with the Lord gathering His desires. In doing so, God rewarded Moses' uninterrupted, unhampered, and focused time with an evident marking of His glory.

As Christians, we should strive daily to have God's glory visibly rest upon us by spending quality time with Him. It was the praise of David in Psalm 21, the admonition of Psalm 89:15-16, and the blessing of Moses in Numbers 6:25-26. Likewise, we too can bask in the Lord's glory. All it would require is that we spend daily uninterrupted and unhampered time in reflection of the Word, prayer, and worship with our God. In doing so, we would then show Him that He is indeed enough for us, and that in His presence we are made whole and secure from the wiles and temptations of this world.

My Brothers and Sisters do you not wish to be kissed by God? More importantly, what does your countenance currently state? Will another member of the body of Christ be able to see the time you have invested in Him? More so, will a lost sheep be able to find your light in a sea of the world's darkness and be drawn to the God in you like a moth to the lamp? Or sadly; will he/she not be able to tell you apart from the guises of the world?

It is my prayer for each of you today that your time with the Lord be renewed and refreshed. I pray that as you recommit and reprioritize your time with Him that His glory rests upon your face and settles within your bones reenergizing you only the way He can. Lastly, it is my prayer that, like Moses, He makes His face to shine upon you and be gracious unto you. I also pray that He gives you peace. I pray this prayer believing now that it has been answered in none other than the matchless name of our Lord and Savior, Jesus Christ. To God be all glory, and honor, and praise, Alleluia!

Quick Trips

Isaiah 3:9   Isaiah 40:5

1 Chronicles 29:11   1 Chronicles 16:9-10

Psalms 3:3   Matthew 28:3

Revelation 1:16

Notes:

You are the God who performs miracles; you display your power among the peoples.

(Psalm 77:14, NIV)

How Great is Our God

Just this past Sunday, I enjoyed several episodes of *Planet Earth* courtesy of the Discovery channel. I watched in awe as the producers rendered detailed insights into earth's animals and their respective habitats. As I traveled with them from the depths of the oceans to the highest mountain tops; and from the moist atmosphere of the rain forest, to the arid air of the deserts; I was truly amazed and even more humbled by the awesomeness of our God. In tears by the time the last episode aired, I had gained yet another perspective of the God whom we serve; and as I sat in humbled reverence I was reminded of a song I used to sing in children's church:

"…so wide, you can't get around it; so low you can't get under it; so high you can't get over it…"

Then it hit me, if I were to change the word *it* in the above verse inserting *Him* instead I would have a close approximation of the greatness of our God detailed in Isaiah 40: 12-26.

As I continued to reflect upon what I had just seen, I was further able to surmise that evidence of His greatness is apparent right here on earth. For example, there are depths within the ocean that man has not yet been able to walk upon; mountains that men have not yet been able to scale or inhabit; as well as tasks that man – even in his wisdom - has not yet been able to complete. Again I say, *so deep; so high; so wide* (His knowledge) – to whom can the Creator be compared?

My brothers and sisters what more evidence do you need to find worthy the Creator, the Source from whence **all good things** are manifested and made whole?

It is my prayer for each of you today that you will undergo a change of perspective with respects to the greatness of our Lord. I pray that through this change, you will be able to better see Him as the creator that He is. As you begin to embrace this mindset, it is my prayer that you will die to yourself daily so that He may increase within you. As He increases, I pray that you will never forget the Source of your renewed faith, peace, and joy. Lastly, it is my prayer that you will depend upon Him for all things trusting that He will supply all your needs according to His riches in heaven. I pray this prayer believing now that it has been answered in none other than the matchless name of our Lord and Savior, Jesus Christ. To God be all glory, and honor, and praise, Alleluia!

Quick Trips

Psalm 33:6, 9	Psalm 89:6
Psalm 103:11	Psalm 139:6
Isaiah 40:15-18	Isaiah 55:9
Acts 17:28	1 Corinthians 2:9

Ephesians 3:15

Notes

Meanwhile the disciples were urging Him, saying, "Rabbi, eat." But He said to them, "I have food to eat that you do not know about." So the disciples were saying to one another, "No one brought Him anything to eat, did he?" Jesus said to them, "My food is to do the will of Him who sent Me and to accomplish His work.
(John 4:31-34, NASB)

Levels of Nourishment

The happiest day of my life was when my children, Dominic and Dominique were born. In an instant I was transformed from being just another individual into being the mother of two precious bundles of joy. For the next few months, I never tired of embracing them, smelling them, or for that matter watching over them as they slept. In addition to the round the clock care they received, they were also treated to lullabies and stories.

Whenever we went out, I would proudly bask in the attention we attained as people commented on either how cute they were, or how exciting it must have been to be the mother of twins. This only further solidified the already perceived significance of my two precious gifts. As such, I labored all the more in caring for them. Succinctly stated, I was in love with that which I had borne.

And so it was in a nurturing environment of love that Dominic and Dominique grew and developed into the two very well trained, loving individuals they are today.

However as the years progressed and they got older, my priorities shifted from that of dressing them in coordinating outfits to teaching them how to be academically successful; from randomly inhaling their essence to teaching them how to be fair in their relationships with others; from singing lullabies to get them to fall asleep to teaching them about God's word. As such, as they grew and matured so did my love for and my instruction to them. As they grew trustworthy in small tasks, I trusted them with bigger ones. As they grew deeper in their relationship with me, I drew them even nearer. As our levels of communication broadened, I shared more and more. And lastly, as I continued to teach them about life and live mine according to the principles of God I sat back and watched how His word took root in their spirits and manifested itself through their thoughts, words, and actions.

In like fashion, my heavenly Father was elated the day I accepted His saving grace. Although He knew me before He formed me in my mother's womb and anointed me prophet to the nations (Jeremiah 1:5) He had to wait until I first took a step toward Him. (Revelation 3:20) When I did, it was one of His happiest moments. Accordingly so and for the next few months, He enveloped me in His love all the while inhaling my essence to remember me as His own; He monitored me while I was awake and watched closely over me as I slept; He sang to me as I transitioned from the world of darkness and lies, into His world of light and truth (John 14:6); and through His word, He made available stories of His love, judgment, and the forgiveness of His people (Luke 6:47). Whenever I went out and people noticed the change in my countenance (Numbers 6:26), He stood next to me beaming with pride for that which He had created. Succinctly stated, He was in love with that which He had redeemed.

However as I grew in Him, His priorities shifted from simply rejoicing over me for my salvation to that of entrusting me with a shared responsibility of kingdom work; from simply having me meditate on the Word for myself, to instructing me in ways to impart the Word to His people (Matthew 5:13); from helping me to identify and hone my spiritual gifts, to using them to minister to others thus doing my part to help in bringing His kingdom to manifestation here on Earth (1 Corinthians 14:12).

Accordingly so, in finding pleasure in my obedience (Romans 16:19), He trusted me with even bigger tasks. As I grew deeper in my relationship with Him, He drew me closer (James 4:8). As our levels of communication deepened, He spoke more frequently (John 10:27). Lastly, as I was exposed to the fullness of joy in Him, he watched as His word took root in my spirit and was fruitfully manifested through my thoughts, my words, and my actions. (Proverbs 16:3) And so it was, in a perpetual cycle of embracing, feeding, coddling, encouraging, and releasing that my heavenly Father has raised me to be a new creation in Him.

Although the above testimony is my own, for some it may serve as an abstract representation of how our heavenly Father nurtures us after we have accepted his invitation of salvation. It would be quite easy for any believer to simply read the above text in the first person and realize just how similar their relationship with Christ is or has been. In honestly reflecting upon this, one might ask him/herself at what level does my experience seem to change and why? On the contrary, one could argue that none of our experiences for that matter would be the same. However, and the question that bears boding; is at what level of nourishment are you at present? Are you still being coddled, or have you been released to do His work? Are you being embraced, or are you currently being encouraged to step out in faith?

It is my prayer for each of you today that you will find the time to reflect upon your level of nourishment with our heavenly Father. I pray that as you reflect upon it in faith that our Lord will speak clearly and reveal truths via His spirit. I also pray that as you put your trust in Him that you will be able to reach full maturity in His spirit. For those of you who may have become stuck or discouraged, I pray for both a refreshing as well as a confidence in Him to fall upon you like you have never experienced before. Lastly, it is my prayer today that we all come to the realization of the part we each must play in bringing others to the fold so that His kingdom will be made manifest here on Earth. I pray this prayer believing now that it has been answered in none other than the matchless name of our Lord and Savior, Jesus Christ. To God be all glory, and honor, and praise, Alleluia!

Quick Trips

Revelation 3:20	Jeremiah 1:5
John 14:6	1 Corinthians 14:12
John 10:27	Luke 6:47
Numbers 6:26	Johns 4:8

Notes

The effective prayer of a righteous man can accomplish much.
(James 5:16(c), NASB)

Prayer Works!

"Sick like a dog," does not begin to describe how I felt last week. On a scale of one to ten the pain that traveled through my body registered at an eleven. In response, my temperature fluctuated back and forth well beyond the one hundred degree mark. The ever present feeling of nausea was made all the more prevalent by my body's natural attempt to warm me, and to top it all off; I could not eat. Nothing stayed down. My energy waned.

Nonetheless, like a tree planted by the water I absolutely refused to be pointed in the general direction of, much less taken to see a doctor. As such, and in true Danielle form; I opted instead to ride it out. Becoming a victim of a BIG, BAD, UGLY injection (Yes, I am a baby!) was simply not an option. Lost somewhere between my mattress and my comforters and left to my own devices, was my only desire. Unbeknownst to me that was about to change…

It was 2:30 Monday afternoon when she called. Naomi, as previously introduced, called to inform me that she was on her way to take me to the doctor. Despite my many protests against her kind, yet unnecessary hospitality; with conviction in hand she demanded that I "Get myself together!" Before I knew it, her voice, no longer in my ear, was replaced with her presence at my doorstep. Already weakened from four days of not eating, I digressed and submitted to her leadership. After all, her mind was already made up.

As we drove, Naomi prayed all the way to the clinic. In true prayer warrior mode, she prayed as she helped me out of the car. She prayed as I registered and she prayed while I waited to be seen. She prayed while I waited for the doctor as well as she prayed while I was being attended to. She prayed even more when the decision was made to send me to another hospital and, if that were not enough; she prayed while she called our Bible study group members asking them to intercede on my behalf. In the end, her prayers were so fervent, so deliberate that they ushered in the holy and powerful presence of the Lord.

As she prayed in tandem with the other group members, I remember there being a release in my spirit that lulled me to sleep. Awakened, after what seemed like a few minutes later; by the sound of conversation I realized that my condition had changed. I felt one hundred percent better! The pains no longer existed, and the fever that had plagued me for days had finally broken. The spirit of infirmity had lost its grip. Alleluia! Noticing that I had stirred, she asked me how I felt. When I responded in the affirmative claiming my healing, she too remarked in excitement about my countenance and how it had changed.

As we both thanked the Lord for His healing mercies it was evident that as promised the fervent prayers of the righteous did indeed usher in my healing. Not only did God work through the faithful prayers of His servant Naomi, but He also heard and answered the prayers of those who interceded on my behalf. To God be the glory!

My Brothers and Sisters, what prayers do you need to have answered today? How fervently are you seeking the Lord in agreement with others for the desires of your heart? It is my prayer for you today that you fervently offer your prayers to the Lord our God. In seeking His will, I pray that your prayers will be deeply rooted in His promises. As you stand in faith upon His word, I pray that you will believe in your heart that your prayers have already been answered. I also pray that you will each take it upon yourselves to intercede for other members of the body of Christ. May the Lord bless your selflessness as you seek to fulfill the greatest commandment of all by loving your neighbor as you love yourself. I pray this prayer believing now that it has been answered in none other than the matchless name of our Lord and Savior, Jesus Christ. To God be all glory, and honor, and praise, Alleluia!

Quick Trips

1 Kings 19-12	Psalm 5:3
Psalm 34:1	Psalm 66:18
Matthew 6:7	Matthew 8:19-20
Luke 6:28	John 9:31
Romans 8:26	James 5:16

Notes

The law of the Lord is perfect, restoring the soul; the testimony of the Lord is sure,

making wise the simple.

(Psalm 19:7 NASB)

Simplicity

One year ago, (2007) the Lord blessed my children and me with a beautiful home. Blinds however; were not part of the deal. Not in a financial position to employ any of the retail blind companies, however the daughter of a man who stressed creative practicality as well as independence, I took it upon myself to design and create my own window treatments.

With a splash of green here from one bargain material store and a dab of brown there from yet another, I was able to produce a welcoming, yet cozy atmosphere in my home. The downside of the treatments however, was such that they did not provide much privacy. During the day, we were able to take full advantage of the natural light that streamed in through our windows – a pleasant plus – however at night the children and I were relegated to putter around in dimly lit rooms until it was time for bed.

It was not until this past Friday that I was introduced to what I believe is the neatest invention - temporary paper blinds. Discovered during casual conversation with a neighbor, I was amazed at not only its cost but of the functionality of the product. Who would have ever thought that the invention of accordion folded butcher-like paper lined with double sided tape would have been such a huge success for people like me whose options were limited? In the end and two days later, a job that was slated to cost thousands of dollars and installed over a period of days was effectually completed in a timeframe of two days and for a fraction of the initial estimated cost. Though the solution was simplistic in nature, the blinds still provided a warm and welcoming atmosphere during the day with the added benefit of privacy during the night.

Cannot the word *simplicity* then be used in much the same way to describe God? Although omniscience, omnipresent, and omnipotent; perfection in simplicity is indeed what God represents. Synonymous to elementary and unsophisticated; uncomplicated and unproblematic, the word simplicity conjures negative images, negative connotations. However, in His infinite wisdom, God is such that He has made not only His word uncomplicated (Psalm 119:130, NASB), but the way to Him unsophisticated (John 14:6 NASB), and his love for us unconditional (Romans 5:8 NASB). A simple fix to all of our problems, calm in times of fear, and strength when we are weak, are all ways God uses to show the simplicity and unfettered perfection of His love.

It is my prayer for you today that you are able to grasp a hold of God's simple yet profound and practical love for you. I pray that in this world of chaos and over superfluous distractions that you will be able to find comfort in His peace as well as understanding in the simple things. Lastly, as you walk in simplicity, I pray that God will grant you revelations pertinent to your life from His infinite treasures of knowledge and wisdom. I pray this prayer believing now that it has been answered in none other than the matchless name of our Lord and Savior, Jesus Christ. To God be all glory, and honor, and praise, Alleluia!

Quick Trips

| Romans 10:9 | Psalm 19:7 |
| Psalm 19:7 | John 14:6 |

Notes

"My God sent His angel and shut the lions' mouths and they have not harmed me, inasmuch as I was found innocent before Him; and also toward you, O king, I have committed no crime."
(Daniel 6:22, NASB)

They Do Exist!

My favorite all time Christmas candy advertisement is the one in which Santa Claus and the Red and Yellow M&M meet each other for the first time. In proclamation of the other's existence, both Santa and the Red M&M faint as they realize the rumors and/or stories they have heard about the other are true. As they exclaim, "They do exist!" they both pass out in sheer disbelief leaving the Yellow M&M towering over them both. It would be interesting to note however whether the Yellow M&M believed all along that Santa was real or whether his lack of excitement was due to his naivety.

Within the past month, I too have come to the realization of something that I knew to exist but have never seen it evidenced so readily in my life. Written in Psalm 91:10-12 David stated that:

> "There shall no evil befall thee, neither shall any plague come nigh thy dwelling. For He shall give his angels charge over thee,

to keep thee in all thy ways. They shall bear thee up in their hands, lest thou dash thy foot against a stone." (NASB)

What a wonderful promise to have, however how much more wonderful to have it applied to the reality of our lives! Allow me to explain.

    An innocent oversight, I inadvertently ran a stop light at a very busy intersection early one morning on my way to work. Although the traffic had already started to flow, it was as if there was an invisible barrier that halted them from moving if only for the few seconds it took me to cross over the intersection. As a result, I was able to sail through the intersection without any imposition from the oncoming traffic. A little shook at first about what could have happened, as well as on the look-out for marked/unmarked police cars, I calmed myself by repeating the words, "He will give His angels charge over me."

    On another occasion, my children and I left the house early one Friday evening to attend our weekly Bible study. When we returned home at midnight, we all fell asleep in front of the TV without thinking to check the doors. On our way upstairs at 2:00 o'clock in the morning we all realized that our home had been unlocked and our home security system disarmed. Again, alarmed with the negative possibilities of what could have happened, I calmed myself by reaffirming His promise, "He will give His angels charge over me."

Thirdly, having experienced the impending doom that comes from watching a vehicle careen towards my car at fifty miles an hour as I sat at a stop sign is nothing compared to the fear I felt knowing that the impact was near only to see the salvation of God as I watched the car stop on a dime, halted by an unseen force. Wrought with fear on this occasion as well, the only comfort I managed to muster came from the Word, "He will give His angels charge over me."

Ripe for the picking as I reacted in the flesh on all three occasions, I had allowed the enemy a slight glimmer of hope. Unfortunately for him however, and because I had been versed in the Word of God; I was able to slam the door in the face of crippling fear by standing firm on the promise, "He will send His angels to guard me in all my ways!"

My Brothers and Sisters, in what situation(s) have you seen the protection of God apparent in your lives through His angels? Upon what rock(s) have they not allowed you to stub your foot?

My prayer for each of you today is a prayer of faith and belief in His angels as well as His protection. I pray that as God sends them to take charge of you that you will be safeguarded both in your coming in and your going out. Lastly, it is my prayer that you will lift up a praise of thanksgiving blessing God for His promise of protection on your lives as well as the charges with whom you have been entrusted. I pray this prayer believing now that it has been answered in none other than the matchless name of our Lord and Savior, Jesus Christ. To God be all glory, and honor, and praise, Alleluia!

Quick Trips

Psalm 34:7	Psalm 91:11-21
Exodus 23:20-23	Acts 5:18-19
Daniel 6:22	Matthew 26:5

Notes

For the love of Christ controls us, having concluded this, that One died for all, therefore all died;
and He died for all, so that they who live might no longer live for themselves, but for Him who died and rose again on their behalf. Therefore from now on we recognize no one according to the flesh; even though we have known Christ according to the flesh, yet now we know Him in this way no longer. Therefore if anyone is in Christ, he is a new creature; the old things passed away; behold, new things have come.
(2 Corinthians 5:14-17, NASB)

Washed Clean

Evidenced through the wondrous parade of budding blossoms and the stir of once hibernating animals, Spring is a season many look forward to as an escape from the brutal temperatures of Winter. As bees buzz in welcome of the budding flowers, and birds whistle while they work; a period of natural renewing is ushered in.

For those of us who suffer with allergies however, spring does come at a cost. Paved roads that were once black during the winter season are now green; cars that were once representative of the visible light spectrum have all been reduced to one color; and people, who other than their allergies have no physical ailments whatsoever, are rendered dependent upon the weather man's daily pollen assessment.

What is worse and seemingly bad news amongst allergy sufferers as well as the self professed neat freaks, pollen gets into everything and is everywhere. Due to its abundance, eyes tear and swell up, noses run, and headaches run rampant as nature announces the arrival of Spring. Jammed into crevice after crevice, and layered upon flat surface after flat surface the pollen seems unrelenting. Try as one might, getting rid of it is virtually impossible. That is, until the rains...

As children we are taught that April showers bring May flowers as we memorize the months of the year. But little did we know Spring showers were also good for washing away pollen. Let us say for example then that the pollen represents our sin, and the rains represent the washing away of said sins through the salvation of our Lord, Jesus. Would it not be fair to say then that indeed the rain is necessary for the continuation of life; that indeed His sacrifice on the cross was required for the forgiveness of sins?

For it is written that we that,

"But we are all as an unclean thing, and all our righteousness are as filthy rags; and we all do fade as a leaf; and our iniquities, like the wind, have taken us away." (Isaiah 64:6, KJV)

But though we are like filthy rags, God in His infinite wisdom and sovereignty provided for us a reprieve for our sins, a lifeline so to speak, through the sacrifice of our His Son, our Lord. Hebrews 10:10-18 states:

> By this will we have been sanctified through the offering of the body of Jesus Christ once for all. Every priest stands daily ministering and offering time after time the same sacrifices, which can never take away sins; but He, having offered one sacrifice for sins for all time, SAT DOWN AT THE RIGHT HAND OF GOD, waiting from that time onward UNTIL HIS ENEMIES BE MADE A FOOTSTOOL FOR HIS FEET. For by one offering He has perfected for all time those who are sanctified. And the Holy Spirit also testifies to us; for after saying, THIS IS THE COVENANT THAT I WILL MAKE WITH THEM:
>
> AFTER THOSE DAYS, SAYS THE LORD:
>
> I WILL PUT MY LAWS UPON THEIR HEART,
>
> AND ON THEIR MIND I WILL WRITE THEM,"
>
> He then says, AND THEIR SINS AND THEIR LAWLESS DEEDS I WILL REMEMBER NO MORE."
>
> Now where there is forgiveness of these things, there is no longer any offering for sin. (NASB)

What a glorious promise to behold, a sacred truth upon which to reflect.

My Brothers and Sisters, it is my prayer for each of you today that the pollen in your life be washed away by the forgiving and refreshing rain of the Lord and Savior, Jesus Christ. It is my prayer that you will seek your salvation by believing in your heart and confessing with your mouth that Jesus Christ is Lord. I pray that you will welcome Him into your heart so that He may fill every crevice with His love, grace, and mercy. In accepting Him, I pray now you will be afflicted no longer by the sins of this world, that you will no longer be allergic to the teaching of the Gospel. It is my prayer that though you were first presented to Him as a filthy rag, you will now – through Him - be made as white as snow. Lastly, I pray that His words may now be etched upon and within your heart and mind as well as on your lips forever more. I pray this prayer believing now that it has been answered in none other than the matchless name of our Lord and Savior, Jesus Christ. To God be all glory, and honor, and praise, Alleluia!

Quick Trips

1 John 1:9	Ephesians 2:8-9
Revelation 3:20	Romans 10:9-10
John 3:16-17	John 8:36
John 10:9	Matthew 24:13
1 Peter 3:18	Acts 2:21

For You formed my inward parts; You wove me in my mother's womb.
I will give thanks to You, for I am fearfully and wonderfully made; wonderful are Your works,
And my soul knows it very well.
(Psalm 139:13-14, NASB)

Wonderfully and Fearfully Made

Much to my mother's very vocal chagrin, I did not maintain the shapely size ten of my high school years well into my later life as she had hoped. And so, between the ages of twenty-three to about thirty five, I suffered continuously with my weight. Stuck in a viscous cycle of weight loss and weight gain, I would often chalk it up to various stressors or stages in my life, i.e. marital bliss, new career happiness, marital stress, pregnancy, baby fat, divorce, marital withdrawal, and although I have only been pregnant once; baby fat - you get the picture. Up and down, and down and up my weight would fluctuate comparable to that of the mercury on a Georgian thermometer during the fall months.

Resolved to do something about it every so often, I would diet and exercise to get off a few pounds in anticipation of some special event or another. However as soon as the event had ended, my supposedly lifelong change would end as well and back would come the weight in all its triumphant glory. Size up after size down over a pitcher of Coke and a package of doughnuts, I would sing, "Woe is me..." to whoever would loan me their ear. Caught somewhere between the melody of my own voice and the sound of my own chewing, I would weave tale after ranting tale of bad genes, bad circumstances, and bad health practices.

Consequently and at the lowest point in my life, my weight had gotten so out of control that I refused to look at myself in the mirror. Traumatized by the daily barrage of beautifully shaped women on TV and in magazines as well as by my own pictures of yore; I fell deeper into the dissatisfaction with my weight. I was simply, in two words, beside myself. But as you probably may have guessed, I resolved to do something about it one last time and fortunately, was successful.

Though the road was long and the journey tough, I struggled through every rice cake and every sit up; I force my way through every carrot stick and plodded through every mile; I slurped through bowl after bowl of sugar free oatmeal while swabbing away pounds and pounds of sweat that, sadly, did not carry over to the scale.

Alleluia and finally, the time surely came when I could proudly say that I had attained my goal weight. Now set in a pleasantly appealing size twelve, the shopping sprees were glorious and the looks upon the faces of friends I hadn't seen in years, priceless! But even though I was successful in conquering my weight issues, I still was not as happy as I thought I would have been. As much as I tried to define myself with makeup, designer clothes, and/or expensive perfumes there was still a lack of confidence that followed me no matter the weight loss. It was not until my relationship with Christ fully develop did I finally realize why.

    Made in God's own image and likeness (Genesis 1:26) we have been patterned after the Master - a similitude of Him. Created an intricate specimen of a plethora of moving parts, systems, and functions He has etched within each of us a physical part of His being. Although we have been made in different shapes, sizes, and colors God is represented in each of us through His image. As such, we each are inherently beautiful.

    Although we cannot see Him, it is His design that we should be able to look into the faces of other human beings and find Him there. More so than others, we should also be able to look at ourselves - at the body that He created - and see Him. "Wonderfully and fearfully made" (Psalm 139: 14) should be the attitude of all of God's counted sheep. We should be secure in the fact that no matter our package size, color, or shape we have been made in the image and likeness of the most high God. (This is not to say however, that we should not be good stewards of our body, but rather that we should not force ourselves to fit into the conforming molds set forth by the world.)

In my obsession with my weight, regardless of whether I was heavy or thin, I was not looking at myself to see God. Rather, I was looking at myself and taking special note of every imperfection, every little flaw I could find. In complaining about one misplaced mole after another, I was not paying homage to God who dwelled within me – the God in whose image and likeness I was made. Instead I was bickering with His creation over trivial non-kingdom matters and making in vain His testament of love to the human race. In not searching for His reflection in the mirror, what I saw was a hollow shell of the actual beautiful creation God had made.

Even though I have not attained my pre-adult life weight, I now am confident, secure, and bold in the fact that I am made in the image and likeness of the most high God. When I look at myself in the mirror, I am happy to say that he is right there staring back at me. More importantly, as is my daily prayer, I know that when others look at me they see Him, too, for I have been fearfully and wonderfully made by Him.

My brothers and sisters, who do others, see when they look at you? Who do you see when you look at yourself?

It is my prayer for each of you today that you no longer allow your image to dictate who you are. I pray that you find God below the surface of your physical insecurities so that His power and confidence may be released within you. Through that release, I pray that others may finally be able to see God in you so they too may be called unto Him. I pray that the next time you look into a mirror to see yourself, that the glory of God is reflected back at you. Lastly, it is my prayer that each of you will be good stewards of your body as it is the temple of the Most High God. I pray this prayer believing now that it has been answered in none other than the matchless name of our Lord and Savior, Jesus Christ. To God be all glory, and honor, and praise, Alleluia!

Quick Trips

1 Peter 3:3-5	1 Corinthians 6:19-20
1 Corinthians 10:31	1 Corinthians 6:9-11
Romans 12:1-2	Leviticus 11:44-45
I John 3:2-3	

Notes

Chapter Two: Praise

If we confess our sins, He is faithful and righteous to forgive us our sins and to cleanse us from all unrighteousness.

(1 John 1:9, NASB)

In the quiet of the night, Lord
When it's just me and You;
I reflect on all the circumstances you have brought me through.
No judgment cast, no sorrows held upon my name to count
As you have washed me white as snow,
No blood stains to be found.
In cleansing me you paved the way for my salvation dear.
I draw You close as You draw me. Together we stand near.
Although Your face I cannot see, Your presence I do feel.
Mold me Lord and make me whole, in worship I do kneel.
In honored adoration to You, Majestic One,
Your glory do I seek to bring, Your will only to be done.
I love you, Lord. I love You, so; Your glory to behold.
More precious that of diamonds, Lord; of silver, or of gold.
Hence,
Consider my lifelong gratitude for Your sacrifice of when
You chose to pay the price to count me as, "Forgiven."

It is my prayer for each of you today that the power of this message takes root within you spirit as you quietly reflect upon the heavy price that was paid for your salvation. It is my prayer for each of you today that this most precious gift is not wasted upon the frivolities this world, but rather that you look upon the heavens beseeching Him to draw you near. Lastly, I pray that as He draws you near you are able to find your purpose in Him through which you will be able to bring others into the fold. I pray this prayer believing now that it has been answered in none other than the matchless name of our Lord and Savior, Jesus Christ. To God be all glory, and honor, and praise, Alleluia!

Let us all now lift up a voice of worship, praise, and thanksgiving to the one, true, and living God! Alleluia!

Quick Trips

2 Chronicles 7:14	Psalm 51:2, 10-12
Proverbs 17:9	Matthew 6:14
Psalm 28:18	Psalm 103:12
Matthew 18:21-22	Matthew 18:35
Hebrews 8:12	Psalm 32:5

For the word of the Lord is right and true; He is faithful in all He does.
The Lord loves righteousness and justice; the earth is full of his unfailing love."
(Psalm 33:4-5, NIV)

I Love You, Lord

When I say, "I Love you, Lord"
I mean I love You as You are.
I have no set expectations…
No selfish motives…
No desire,
Other than to let you know how much
I love you.

It is my prayer for each of you today that you will, "Love the Lord your God with all your heart and with all your soul and with all your might." (Deuteronomy 6:5, NASB) Standing on the promise of Matthew 16:19, I pray now that if there be any selfish motives and desires for loving Him that they will be stripped and loosed in the precious name of our Lord and Savior, Jesus Christ. In its place, I pray that a love pure and abounding in trust, faith, and hope in Him be bound upon you. Lastly, it is my prayer that your renewed love will be pleasing and acceptable unto Him as a living sacrifice. I pray this prayer believing now that it has been answered in none other than the matchless name of our Lord and Savior, Jesus Christ. To God be all glory, and honor, and praise, Alleluia!

Notes

"All the earth will worship You, and will sing praises to You;
They will sing praises to Your name."
Selah.
(Psalm 66:4, NIV)

Nature Praise

The flowers lift their petals high in adoration, Lord.
Their face to the sun they drink You in, their sustenance from above.
The birds an endless praise they sing, of sweet, sweet melodies.
As they themselves they lift You up in wanting just to please.
The trees they bow to worship You as you whisper in the wind,
The grass stretch to their tallest stance again and yet again.
The crickets of the wild exclaim their praise in chirps to You
And the skies above reveal their love in the clearest shades of blue.
All of nature extols you Lord, All of nature sings,
All of nature buzzes with excitement of the King.
Praise you, Lord!

I pray the blessings of Numbers 6: 24 – 26 on each of you today:

"The Lord bless you, and keep you;
 The Lord make His face shine on you,
  And be gracious to you;
 The Lord lift up His countenance on you,
  And give you peace."

I pray this prayer believing now that it has been answered in none other than the matchless name of our Lord and Savior, Jesus Christ. To God be all glory, and honor, and praise, Alleluia!

Quick Trips

Psalm 7:17	Psalm 28:6-7
Psalm 118:28-29	Psalms 89:6
Jeremiah 33:11	Philippians 4:4
1 Thessalonians 5:16	1 Peter 1:8
Luke 18:43	Revelation 19:5

Notes

_____
_____
_____
_____
_____

This is the day which the LORD has made; let us rejoice and be glad in it.

(Psalm 118:24, NASB)

Today...

How often is it that we find someone?
Whose presence brings light to our lives?
Who with just a touch or a fleeting glance
Can silence the most deafening noise?
How often is it that we are inspired
By a Spirit who defines life?
Whose courage withstands the blunt of all fears?
Whose closeness gives us a high?
How often is it that a love endures all,
In a pure and unprovoked state
While sustaining the hearts in which it remains
Until reunited with its mate?
How often is it that Life renews life –
The gift that surpasses all others,
To share, to laugh, to love, and to cry
With our friends our sisters, and brothers?
Today is upon us,

> New mercies unfold
> Embracing the promise
> Of blessings foretold...
> "For I know the plans I have for you," thus said the Lord.
> Bless your Holy name!

As you cleave to His promise of never leaving or forsaking you, my prayer this morning is simply this: That you will rejoice in this day that the Lord has made thanking Him yet again for a new dawning of grace and mercy. I pray this prayer believing now that it has been answered in none other than the matchless name of our Lord and Savior, Jesus Christ. To God be all glory, and honor, and praise, Alleluia!

Notes

_____
_____
_____
_____
_____
_____
_____
_____

Sing to Him, sing praises to Him; speak of all His wonders.
(1 Chronicles 16:9, NASB)

Whooping It Up for the Lord!

When I was a little girl, I dreamed of living a full-fledged adult life including, but not limited to going to the clubs. As a teenager, my club curiosity only deepened when I adopted BET as one my favorite past times. As I began my university days, I was able to attend several house parties as well as club events with my parents' permission. Finally, as an adult I would occasionally attend club functions with a few of my friends to celebrate one life event or another. When I got saved however, and for all intent and purposes; I thought that my club/party days were over. However, nothing could have been further from the truth.

Last night, I attended a party unlike any I have ever experienced. The music was intense and the guests were filled with excitement; smoke machines produced an atmosphere conducive for intimate encounters and the dim lighting perfect for setting the mood. From the atmosphere alone, I anticipated nothing less than a heavenly encounter and became even more hopeful as there was already a spirit of expectancy flowing freely throughout the room. The crowd went wild as the MC stepped out onto the stage to get the party started and as they say, "The rest was history." A healing and deliverance gathering tied to a corporate period of prayer and seeking God's will, some experienced the Lord like never before. In the end, many received their deliverance from stifling strongholds, while still others claimed their healing in the name of Jesus.

As a corporate body, we whooped it up for the Lord. Free in our worship and oblivious to our surroundings, many danced within the aisles singing praises unto the Lord. Others ran as the spirit of the living God embraced them, while still others fell to floor to worship in the splendor of the Lord that had settled upon the room. Others simply wept. For roughly an hour and a half, approximately one thousand people sought after Him in fervent desire. As the party ended and the crowd started to disperse, it was obvious that the glory of the Lord was visited upon each and every person in attendance that evening. Indeed, it was a beautiful sight. In short, the service was reminiscent to that of the praise and worship offered to the Lord by King David and the Israelites upon the return of the Ark of the Covenant (2 Samuel 6.)

It was obvious that the Lord was pleased with last night's corporate gathering; however I am positive that He have would absolutely and positively appreciate us *whooping it up* with Him every so often by ourselves. Not at all discounting the power of corporate prayer/or worship, but the Lord desires to hear our individual voices of praise and thanksgiving as often as possible as well.

Evidenced in his psalms, David recognized this and suggested several situations when it was appropriate to praise the Lord. Here are a few examples: We are to praise Him while entering into His gates (Psalm 100:4, NASB), we are to praise Him through our singing (Psalm 69:30, NASB), we are also supposed to praise Him when we are down (Psalm 43:5, NASB). As a matter of fact we were created for this exact purpose. Accordingly so and from this moment on, let us make it a habit to praise Him unceasingly no matter the circumstance.
(1 Thessalonians 5:16-18, NASB) Praise does indeed have its rewards, however none of which is greater than simply loving on our Daddy up in heaven.

It is my prayer for you today that He may inhabit your praise at all times. As you continue to diligently seek Him, it is my prayer that *whooping it up with the Lord* will become your favorite pass time, second to none. As your faith grows, I pray that you will stand firm on His promises. Lastly, I pray that your continued praise and worship will usher you into a new season of favor as He graciously smiles upon you. I pray this prayer believing now that it has been answered in none other than the matchless name of our Lord and Savior, Jesus Christ. To God be all glory, and honor, and praise, Alleluia!

Quick Trips

1 Chronicles 29:11-13	Philippians 4:4
Philippians 4:8	Jeremiah 33:11
Psalm 7:17	Psalm 33:1-5
Matthew 21:16	Romans 5:11
1 Corinthians 4:5

Notes

Chapter Three:

Counsel

For this reason also, God highly exalted Him, and bestowed on Him the name which is above every name, so that at the name of Jesus EVERY KNEE WILL BOW, of those who are in heaven and on earth and under the earth, and that every tongue will confess that Jesus Christ is Lord, to the glory of God the Father.
(Philippians 2:9-11, NASB)

All in His Name

In addition to the many other wonderful gifts God has bestowed us, He has also given us the blessed gift of His name. Depicted in *It's All in Your Name,* Cece Winans made it very clear the many things we can claim in the name of Jesus – i.e. deliverance, healing, security, peace, and/or provision just to name a few. Simply stated, the power of His name is such that when we call, no matter the reason; He comes.

II Corinthians 14:11 shows us just how easy it is for us to talk to the Lord in seeking His assistance.

> "Then Asa called to the LORD his God and said," "LORD, there is no one like you to help the powerless against the mighty. Help us, O LORD our God, for we rely on you, and in your name we

> have come against this vast army. O LORD, you are our God; do not let man prevail against you."

Further, in Psalm 99:6 it is made evident that the Lord responds whenever His name is called.

> "Moses and Aaron were among his priests, Samuel was among those who called on his name; they called on the LORD and he answered them."

Lastly, in Joel 2:32 we find a word from God himself saying,

> "And everyone who calls on the name of the LORD will be saved; for on Mount Zion and in Jerusalem there will be deliverance, as the LORD has said, among the survivors whom the LORD calls."

Isn't that a beautiful thought? To know that our God is simply a whisper away if ever we needed Him.

The problem with the use of this gift however arises when we choose to call on the name of the Lord in vain as an expression of frustration as opposed to an expression of love; as an expression of disgust as opposed to one of praise; or even as an expression of sarcasm as opposed to one of worship, these are the times when we call on Him not needing anything at all. This grieves Him.

Evidenced in Exodus 20:7 and Deuteronomy 5:11, the Bible warns against it twice saying,

"Thou shalt not take the name of the LORD thy God in vain; for the LORD will not hold him guiltless that taketh his name in vain." (NKJ)

The God we serve is a loving and merciful God who shows himself present and mighty at the calling of His name. Accordingly so, the name of the Lord is only to be used in times of need, worship, praise, outreach, testimony, or deliverance. It should never be used as an expression to show disgust, lust, sarcasm, or impatience. Can you honestly, after being warned; find yourself laying waste to that most glorious and precious gift?

It is my prayer for you today that you will first repent of calling the Lord's name in vain. I pray that you will then never be party to that type of behavior again. It is my prayer that as you use His name correctly, He will respond accordingly to the request you have faithfully uttered. Finally, I pray the blessing of the Lord upon your lives as you continue to walk with and in Him. I pray this prayer believing that it has been answered in none other than the matchless name of our Lord and Savior, Jesus Christ our Savior. To God be all glory, honor, and praise, Alleluia!

Quick Trips

1 John 2:1   Matthew 9:15
1 Peter 5:4   Jeremiah 8:18

Romans 11:26 Matthew 1:23
Psalm 48:14 Isaiah 41:14, 42:1

For you know very well that the day of the Lord will come like a thief in the night. While people are saying, "Peace and safety," destruction will come on them suddenly, as labor pains on a pregnant woman, and they will not escape. But you, brothers, are not in darkness so that this day should surprise you like a thief.
(1 Thessalonians 5:2-4, NIV)

Are You Ready?

Well, it finally happened… After eighteen years of successfully avoiding a potentially embarrassing confrontation, it eventually came to pass. Not without the pomp and circumstance, of course; however with the angst with which I had anticipated…

I was on my way home one afternoon. It was 3:55 when I noticed the flashing blue lights behind me. Undeniably, my first response was to switch lanes so as to get out of the way of the persistent blue lights. But, as I flashed my indicator to signal that I was about to switch lanes, so did the source of the blue lights.

"Oh darn," I sighed. "I can't believe I am being pulled over."

Just as I had practiced, I began to take mental inventory of all the documents I would have to show upon request. After all, I had watched enough crime TV to know what to expect.

"License? Check! Insurance card? Check! Tags? Ugh!" My thirty – eighth birthday had passed just four days earlier (something else I didn't expect to happen as soon as it did) and with it the deadline for renewing my tags.

As I waited for the officer to approach my now parked car, I prayed silently asking not to be overcome with fear or nervous energy. No sooner had I prayed than I was at peace. As a result of my prayers, I was also reminded of a conversation I had had a week prior in which I was told that I had a thirty day grace period for renewing my tags.

Now at peace and singing the Lord's praises, I cordially greeted the officer as he approached my window. After he responded in kind, he proceeded to ask about – yup, you guessed it – the status of my registration. When I countered that indeed my birthday had already passed but that I was still within the thirty day grace period, he responded that he was not aware of any such ordinance.

With my license in hand, he proceeded to his car to inquire of his partner. Approximately five minutes later, he returned to confirm that indeed I was right. Nonetheless, he still issued me a warning. In the end, I thanked him kindly for his time, and I drove off thanking God for the peace that was placed upon my heart as well as the grace I had received.

On the way home however, the encounter got me thinking about the end. Would I be ready when the Lord comes? More so, would I nonchalantly check things off in my mind as I waited to stand before Him in judgment?

"Holy and righteous life? Check. Intimate relationship with Christ? Check. Service? Check. Faith and surrender in **ALL** things? Ugh!"

My brothers and sisters will you be ready? It is written, "But of that day and hour no one knows, not even the angels of heaven, nor the Son, but the Father alone." (Matthew 24:36, NASB) Accordingly so, will you be able to peacefully state, "Well, the day is finally here. Thousands of years after His promise of return, here He stands in all His glory." Again I ask, "Are you ready?"

It is my prayer for each of you today that you will make the time to prepare for your eternal life with our heavenly Father. As always, I pray that you will submit to the leading of the Holy Spirit as He guides you in repentance. I pray your sins may be removed from you as far as the east is from the west (Psalm 103:12) so that they may no longer be like an anchor around your neck. Lastly, as your transgressions are forgiven I pray that you will seize a hold of your salvation thereby committing to living a life that is pleasing unto Him so that you will be well prepared to stand blameless before Him even prior to Judgment Day. I pray this prayer believing now that it has been answered in none other than the matchless name of our Lord and Savior, Jesus Christ. To God be all glory, and honor, and praise, Alleluia!

Quick Trips

Matthew 16:27-28   Matthew 24:27, 29-31
Matthew 24:34   Matthew 25:1-13
Acts 1:11   1 John 3:2-3

Notes

Therefore let us not judge one another anymore, but rather determine this-- not to put an obstacle or a stumbling block in a brother's way."

(Romans 14:13, NASB)

By What Measure?

Throughout the years, my father has warned me about pretentiously holding others to my standards.

"Danie," he would always begin, "we are not all the same. Everyone has a different way of doing things. Why do you think your way is best?"

Despite my frequent protests however, he would always stand his ground.

"How would you feel if someone, whose standards were higher than yours, judged your shortfalls?"

"Hmmm," I would respond. "I wouldn't like it very much."

"Of course you wouldn't," he would always end.

It was not until this morning's devotional that I fully understood the depth and breadth of my father's admonitions. Led to Matthew 7: 1-2 which states,

> "Do not judge so that you will not be judged. For in the way you judge, you will be judged; and by your standard of measure, it will be measured to you," (NASB)

I was left to ponder any words, thoughts, or actions that could have posed judgment upon anyone with whom I had interacted in the past couple of weeks. Though not malicious in nature, there had been many.

In retrospect, I had judged when I compared a parent's methods of correcting their child in comparison to my own methods; I had judged when I questioned the priorities of a parent who opted to clothe their child as opposed to purchasing a much needed new pair of glasses; I had judged when I chose to discontinue a friendship because of the hurtful nature of the words and/or actions imposed. I had judged without first knowing the causes by which their actions were motivated. I had judged without even asking of and/or listening to their reasoning for doing the things they did. As I recounted those many thoughts, I had no other choice than to immediately repent, and ask forgiveness for my wicked judgmental ways.

My Brothers and Sisters, is there anyone whom you have judged based on their life's circumstance, status, or lack thereof? Is there anyone whom you have chosen not to forgive for the way you have been treated? Most importantly, by what measure will you be judged in return?

It is my prayer for each of you today that you first reflect upon the log that is stuck in your eye prior to seeking the splinter in your neighbor's. (Luke 6:41) In doing so, I pray that your judgment of others will cease so that you may not be measured in turn by the same lengths you have imposed. More so, it is my prayer that you will seek the Lord's forgiveness as you repent of your wicked, judgmental ways. With judgment removed, I pray that you will be able to see the beauty of God in all of His people no matter their weaknesses, life's circumstance, or short comings. Lastly, I pray that you will choose now to minister to others in a loving way as you seek to remove stumbling blocks that hinder them from coming to and surrendering to Christ. I pray this prayer believing now that it has been answered in none other than the matchless name of our Lord and Savior, Jesus Christ. To God be all glory, and honor, and praise, Alleluia!

Quick Trips

Luke 6:31, 37	Romans 2:1-3
Romans 14:1-13	1 Corinthians 4:3-4
2 Corinthians 5:10	Galatians 5:14

Let no one say when he is tempted, "I am being tempted by God"; for God cannot be tempted by evil, and He Himself does not tempt anyone. But each one is tempted when he is carried away and enticed by his own lust.

(James 1:13-14 NASB)

How Low Can You Go?

Everyone has a standard. Whether it is a high standard for that which one seeks, or a standard that dictates what one will never accept; we all maintain a level to which we uphold ourselves as well as portray to those around us. The problem with standards however, is that they seem to easily swing pendulously from one end of the spectrum to the next based upon what day of the week it is, the company we keep, or the desires of our hearts on any given matter. Comprised sometimes of false pride, but also based upon aspirations, hopes, opportunity, and dreams; standards are the things of which nightmares can be made, a breeding ground for disappointment.

For example, one might decide to remain celibate until marriage prior to finding a mate, however; once a proposal has been attained that standard may be lowered to the convenient excuse of, "We are getting married anyway." Likewise, someone who has had a clear concept of the mate they seek would - after years of being alone - choose to abandon their preconceived standard in an effort to speed the process along as opposed to simply waiting on the Lord.

Accordingly so, one of my paternal grandmother's favorite saying was, "Before none, any." Applied to the afore mentioned example of lowering one's standard as opposed to maintaining one's initial desires, this old adage can be applied to other areas of our lives as well. Jobs, purchases, churches, friends, behavior, or for that matter conversations are all areas in which we all lower our standards from time to time in an effort to fit in. The problem with this however is as time progresses the high standards to which we once adhered gets lowered to the point where our actions, decisions, and/or relationships are no longer reflective of the commandments of the Lord – the Law to which we ought to abide.

As Christians, it is then our responsibility to live first as though unto the Lord, but also as a living example – a city set high on a hill (Matthew 5:14-16) – for all to see the living God manifested through us. As Christians, it then becomes our responsibility to stand for something, lest we fall for anything – the something being the God in whom we live, breathe, and have our being (Acts 17:28); the *anything* being the guises of the enemy and the many ways he devises to divide and conquer God's people.

The good news today my Brothers and Sisters is that our Lord – the one through whom we are saved – is the same yesterday, today, and forever (Hebrews 13:8.) As should our standards, He never changes. As such, I encourage you to stand firm for what you know is right, so that you will not perish (Ephesians 6:10-11.) Rebuke the devil for your own sakes, and he will flee (James 4:7.)

It is my prayer for each of you today that you will first repent for the lowering of any standards that enabled you to exist contrary to the word of God. It is my prayer that through your repentance the Lord will give you the grace necessary to resist any additional temptations or attacks from the enemy that may come your way. I further pray discernment upon you so that you will be able to eat the meat necessary for your spiritual growth and edification and spit out the bones not vital to your spiritual nurturing. I pray now that the peace of the Lord that is within us all may surround you as you reflect upon the greatness, albeit the sameness of our God as you revel in the knowledge that He never changes. I pray this prayer believing now that it has been answered in none other than the matchless name of our Lord and Savior, Jesus Christ. To God be all glory, and honor, and praise, Alleluia!

Quick Notes

Exodus 20:2-17   Romans 12:1-2

Deuteronomy 30:19   John 15:19

1 John 2:15

Notes

> Pride goes before destruction, and a haughty spirit before stumbling.
>
> (Proverbs 16:18, NASB)

Humble and Contrite

As a young child my father would often tease me about being too sensitive. It did not take much to make me cry. My eyes would well up with sincere tears of concern at the sight of a stray dog, a person in a wheel chair, or while watching as an animal of prey would fall victim to its natural predator on the local PBS channel. Jokingly my father would always query in jest about the tears I had to spare.

What he did not know however was that my tears also served a dubious purpose the object of which was to escape my parents' anger - as a tool to circumvent their justifiable wrath whenever any of my ill-advised actions were brought to light. As such, I would immediately begin to tear up at either the threat of a spanking, a disconcerted "Hmph" from my mother complete with her 'under the eyebrow look' (my fellow Caribbean folk and/or descendants of said know of what I speak), or an inkling that my ruse had been found out. Driven by fear and as opposed to subjecting myself to the consequences of my actions I would opt instead to *act* them out of their anger.

Seemingly humble and contrite, I would plead my case. As a precursor to the blows I know I was about to receive, the tears would form easily and fall freely as I recounted motive after motive, mistake after mistake – anything to distract them from the task at hand. Ranging from compliments to outright denial of the alleged incident the intensity with which I pleaded would wax and wane in response to the severity of my parents' anger and/or interest in what I had to say. Accordingly so, if their anger waned, so did the passion with which I argued as I tried desperately to smooth them over. On the other hand, if their anger worsened the tears would fall even quicker as my argument, and ultimate desperation was kicked up notch.

But it was not until I grew older and began to interact on a higher level of communication with my parents did I come to realize the importance of not only confessing my sins, but of sincerely apologizing for my infractions as well as asking their forgiveness. I subsequently learned that my parents were more proned to listen to me as I dutifully and sincerely *fessed* up, repented of, and asked for their forgiveness. It was ultimately during these times that I learned the power of repentance. Not as it is more readily used as simply an obligatory tool to make more palatable one's interactions with others, but rather as our heavenly Father intended - a sincere token of acknowledgement and remorse for the wrongs we have done. By learning to stand broken before those whom we offend, we thereby activate - in faith – due forgiveness, mercy, and grace. Is this not the same pattern of repentance our heavenly Father would have us to follow?

Isaiah 66:2 states:

> "For My hand made all these things, thus all these things came into being," declares the LORD. But to this one I will look, to him who is humble and contrite of spirit, and who trembles at My word." (NASB)

My brothers and sisters, would the one who dwells in the high and holy place wish to dwell within your heart to revive it? (Isaiah 57:15) Or is there no room for Him because of the false pride and denial that has been stored there?

It is my prayer for each of you today that you will be able to vanquish all things that are prideful within you lest you stumble and be destroyed. It is my prayer that you will instead choose to assume a humble and contrite demeanor releasing everyone and everything by which you were once offended. Lastly, as you make yourself one of those upon who God looks, I pray that He will come to dwell within you, reviving your heart, all the while building you up so that you may be filled with His unending peace and joy. I pray this prayer believing now that it has been answered in none other than the matchless name of our Lord and Savior, Jesus Christ. To God be all glory, and honor, and praise, Alleluia!

Quick Trips

Proverbs 3:34	Proverbs 16:19
Proverbs 22:4	Psalm 51:17
Matthew 11:29	Matthew 23:12
James 4:6	2 Corinthians 7:10
Revelation 3:19	

Notes

The good man out of the good treasure of his heart brings forth what is good; and the evil man out of the evil treasure brings forth what is evil; for his mouth speaks from that which fills his heart.
(Luke 6:45, NASB)

Of What Does Your Heart Speak?

A few years ago, I worked with a supervisor who was very caustic with her words. To us, the position of power made her believe she had the ability to speak to us however she chose. Almost as if it were an item on her To Do List, she did not think twice about making audible, negative comments about those around her. If that were not enough, she also took pleasure in sarcastically demeaning whomever she spoke with using her academic and experiential prowess as an excuse. At one point, her reputation had gotten so bad that she became known on campus as, "the fastest way to clear the room." As a result of her tempestuous behavior, she was lonely. And, it was this perpetual loneliness that eventually made her even more bitter.

What we did not know then, but later found out, was that she had been suffering a rough patch in her marriage as well as other resentments and regrets in her personal life. Because of this, she reflected the unhappiness she harbored in her heart to those in closest proximity – us.

Quite the contrary and on the same job, I also worked with a lady who could melt butter with her words. She was warm, inviting, and full of good cheer. She always had a kind word of encouragement or praise for those who needed it, and she frequently quoted scriptures in alignment to one's need at the time. Now that I think about it, she was the one to whom many ran in an effort to counteract the poisonous effects of dealing with our supervisor. In hindsight, she was spirit filled.

Likewise, what we did not know then but later found out was that she had been diagnosed with breast cancer. Moreover, her family had almost been on the brink of financial ruin due to her disease. However, and as opposed to brooding, she chose instead to cultivate an intimate and beautiful relationship with the Lord. As a result, her love for Him and the abundance of joy that filled her heart was made all the more obvious in her interactions with us.

My Brothers and Sisters what fills your heart? Is it the love, faith, hope, and reverence for our Lord, God; or is it doubt, uncertainty, fear, malice, or disdain for your fellow man? In reflection, what evidence is brought forth in your words?

It is my prayer for you today that the spirit of the Lord inhabits your heart. I pray a supernatural refreshing of joy upon you right now. It is my prayer that as He fills your temple the overflow will be made evident to all those around you. Lastly, I pray that those with whom you come into contact will recognize who and Whose you are by your actions, thoughts, and words. I pray this prayer believing now that it has been answered in none other than the matchless name of our Lord and Savior, Jesus Christ. To God be all glory, and honor, and praise, Alleluia!

Quick Trips

Proverbs 4:23	Proverbs 14:30
Proverbs 15:13	Proverbs 17:22
Proverbs 27:19	Proverbs 28:14
Matthew 12:34	Matthew 15:18-19
Matthew 22:37	Luke 21:34
Romans 10:9-10	Ephesians 1:18

Notes

> There is a way which seems right to a man,
> But its end is the way of death.
> (Proverbs 16:25, NASB)

Running towards Destruction

This morning, I was reminded of the movie Twister which aired in theaters in the spring of 1996. The movie depicted two competing teams of meteorologists whose job it was to chase tornadoes in an attempt to gather new and improved data for measuring the intensity, as well as predicting the patterns of movement in tornadoes. In an effort to gain their information, and while everyone else ran in the opposite direction; the two teams ran toward the storms braving destruction and mayhem, debris, flying cows, and torrential winds. Although their actions may have been deemed chivalrous by their fellow meteorologists; that said recklessness is what led to the loss of lives.

Very abstractly then, let us take that same scenario and apply it to the lives of many who, under the auspices of life, are running towards a similar yet more eternal destruction. In the frenzy of living in the moment, meeting self ordained purposes and goals; their eyes have been closed, their hearts hardened to the truths of the living God. As they busy themselves in worldly tasks, i.e. sin - they fail to notice signs along the way that point in the opposite direction, or worse, others who have seen and acknowledged said signs heeding the warning in the hopes of reaping the harvest of an eternal life. Unbeknownst to them however, and as they ignore each warning; they are well on their way to forfeiting their place in eternity with their heavenly Father. As they continue to participate in the things that grieve God's heart, their hearts in turn are hardened. (Proverbs 6:16-19, 1 Corinthians 6:9-10, 1Timothy 4: 2)

Matthew 7:13-14 encourages us to,

> Enter through the narrow gate; for the gate is wide and the way is broad that leads to destruction, and there are many who enter through it. "For the gate is small and the way is narrow that leads to life, and there are few who find it. (NASB)

Yet even though it is written, many chose to feed the desires of their flesh as opposed to living in the spirit. My Brothers and Sisters, upon what road are you traveling? Are you walking on the broad path heading toward the eternal destruction of your soul, or are you earnestly seeking the narrow gate?

It is my prayer for each of you today that you seek in earnest the narrow gate. I pray that your eyes will be opened to see the directional signs, your ears opened to hear the word of the living God, and your hearts softened to receive His counsel. I pray now that you will forego the enemy's sentence to death opting instead to choose eternal life whilst not laying waste to the Sacrifice that was made for us. Lastly, it is my prayer that your spirits will come to full attention and raise up a standard against your flesh and the things of this world. I pray this prayer believing now that it has been answered in none other than the matchless name of our Lord and Savior, Jesus Christ. To God be all glory, and honor, and praise, Alleluia!

Quick Trips

Proverbs 19:16	Jeremiah 7: 23
Jeremiah 16:12	Galatians 5:7
1 John 2:4-5	2 John 1:9
Hebrews 3:12-14	1 Samuel 12:14
Deuteronomy 5:29	Revelation 3:3
Revelation 3:20	

Notes

Now he who was betraying Him had given them a signal, saying, "Whomever I kiss, He is the one; seize Him and lead Him away under guard." After coming, Judas immediately went to Him, saying, "Rabbi!" and kissed Him. They laid hands on Him and seized Him.

(Mark 14:44-46, NASB)

The Beauty of Betrayal

As defined by the Cambridge Online dictionary, to betray means *to not be loyal to your country or a person, often by doing something harmful.* Used frequently throughout the airwaves, it is a word that many a soap opera, soul ballad, or first rate movie is founded upon. As such, and if not already victim to this vicious element; one would tend to believe that the romanticist portrayal of betrayal is evidenced only in the shadows of the theater downgraded only to fantasy as the curtains fall and applause fills the room.

Quite the contrary, *betrayal* can be found in many a local subdivision and apartment complex; in the workplace and schoolhouse; or for that matter, in many a marriages and friendships. More so, it is the basis upon which real families are ripped apart, friendships are led to the wayside, and many a betrayed person is left to repeatedly ask themselves in a barrage of negative emotions: "What did I do to deserve this?" "Was I not good enough? or What did I not do?" Broken and all forlorn, most promise that they would never love, marry, or befriend any one again and, until they have been delivered from said rejection; often mope off into the sunset quite the opposite of the romantic portrayal of doing so to a life of happily ever after.

Betrayal however, is not a newly devised concept. Jesus was betrayed in the garden of Gethsemane by Judas of Iscariot for thirty pieces of silver. Betrayed by an act of endearment, Judas of Iscariot identified Jesus with a kiss. The soldiers then turned Him over to Pontius Pilate (Matthew 26:46 – 48.) Although necessary to fulfill the scripture, can any one of us imagine the torment Jesus must have felt being led to His enemies at the hands of one of His disciples? Possibly riddled with anxiety, Jesus could have very easily moped off into the sunset, begged for mercy, or worse refused to die on the cross for us. Fortunately for us, He did none of those things.

Knowing full well that any action other than His death on the cross would have robbed us of the gift of salvation, Jesus forgave them Judas of his trespass, choose to place His feelings aside, and continued with God's perfect will for His life. In pretty much the same way, though hurt; we too should also forgive those who trespass against us. In doing so, we will then be able to repent of our ill feelings for the person(s) responsible and be able to continue along with God's perfect will for our lives.

According to His word, we are instructed to forgive freely and continually. Evidenced in Matthew 6:14-15 as well as in Matthew 18:21-22 we see the reason for the forgiveness of others in addition to the amount of times we should forgive those who offend us.

> "For if ye forgive men their trespasses, your heavenly Father will also forgive you: but if ye forgive not men their trespasses, neither will your Father forgive your trespasses." (Matthew 6:14-15, KJV)

> "Then Peter came and said to Him, "Lord, how often shall my brother sin against me and I forgive Him? Up to seven times?" Jesus said to him, I do not say to you, up to seven times, but up to seventy times seven." (Matthew 18: 21-22, NASB)

Wounded by betrayal, I know firsthand the range of emotions associated with disloyalty. But in utilizing Jesus' mandate of forgiveness, I have been able to let go of past hurts and inclinations of rejection. I would be a liar however, if I did not say that letting go was indeed painful. But the pain I endured was nothing compared to the price my Lord and Savior, Jesus Christ paid for my salvation. Accordingly so, I can now truly say that had it not been for me forgiving those who trespassed against me I would not be presently walking in God's perfect will for my life.

As such my Brothers and Sisters what past hurts or rejections are hindering you from His perfect will for your life? What painful memory or un-forgiven person is causing you to mope off into the sunset as opposed to living happily ever after in Christ?

It is my prayer for each of you today that you will be able to forgive your fellow man his trespasses. I also pray that in forgiving them, you will be able to repent of any ill will towards your fellow man. I pray that in surrendering all disappointments you will be able to walk in God's perfect will for your life. Lastly, I pray that with your renewed faith you will be able to pursue love and/or friendships once more according to the pure and unconditional love of our heavenly Father. I pray this prayer believing now that it has been answered in none other than the matchless name of our Lord and Savior, Jesus Christ. To God be all glory, and honor, and praise, Alleluia!

Quick Trips

Matthew 6:14	Matthew 18:35
Colossians 2.12	Colossians 3:13
Mark 11:25	Hebrews 8:12, 17-18

All Scripture is inspired by God and profitable for teaching, for reproof, for correction, for training in righteousness; so that the man of God may be adequate, equipped for every good work.
(2 Timothy 3:16-17, NASB)

The Feeding of Spirits

One of my all time favorite children's stories is Eric Carle's, *Very Hungry Caterpillar*. In it, he details the four stages in the life cycle of a caterpillar. From egg to caterpillar and then from cocoon to butterfly, Mr. Carle follows the caterpillar throughout its life. Using the days of the week as a spring board for his story and his very unusual, yet vibrant illustrations as the backdrop, Mr. Carle track's the caterpillar's life from its inception through to its beautiful metamorphosis.

Despite the caterpillar's lowly beginning as an egg on Monday and its graceful emergence as a butterfly on Sunday; the majority of its life – Tuesday through to Saturday - is spent eating. As soon as the caterpillar hatched, he ate. And. He did not stop eating until he had engorged himself on the goodness of everything that was around him, i.e. plums, oranges, strawberries, apples, sausages, lollipops, etc. In the end it was his infernal desire to eat compounded with his insatiable eating that got him through to his transition of becoming a new creation – a butterfly.

As Christians, we too are like that caterpillar. The day we accept Jesus as our personal Lord and Savior signifies the day when we are hatched, or born again. And. The day we transform into the new creation He intended for us to be signifies the day we emerge from our cocoon as a butterfly. What is important to note however is that the time we spend getting from the egg stage to the butterfly stage depends solely upon our insatiable urge to eat, the spiritual foods we ought to gorge ourselves upon. For example, we feed our bodies with food when we are physically hungry, and we feed our desires (souls) when the need arrives. Why then do we as Christians tend to overlook the feeding of our spirits, the part of us in which the living God dwells?

1 Thessalonians 5:23 clearly states that we are made up of three parts - spirit, soul, and body – our spirit being the part of us that is listed first. Would it then not be prudent to place more emphasis upon feeding that part of us that is listed first in the Word? Indeed it should, for Hebrews 4:12 states,

> For the word of God is living and active and sharper than any two-edged sword, and piercing as far as the division of soul and spirit, of both joints and marrow, and able to judge the thoughts and intentions of the heart. (NASB)

The above referenced scripture makes it very clear then that the purpose of God's living word is to separate and judge both the intentions and the thoughts of man's heart. In an effort to get this return for our time simply requires of us that we immerse ourselves in and engorge our spirits upon the word of God. By doing this the living word of God will be able to grow exponentially within us ultimately constructing stronger spirits so that the deceitful intentions and thoughts of our heart and soul will have no other choice than to fall into direct order with the teachings and commandments of the Lord.

My Brothers and Sisters, have you fed your spirits today? Have you spent time in God's presence via the Word? It is only with spending time in the Word that you will be able to emerge the new creation God intended for you to be.

It is my prayer for each of you today that you are able to set aside a daily designated time for the feeding of your spirit. I pray that as you immerse yourself in the Word that your spirit will grow in leaps and bounds as you embrace the Father's teachings. As your soul and flesh become subdued to the whiles of the world I pray that they too will submit to the leading of the spirit so that you may stand blameless before the Lord upon His return. Lastly, it is my prayer that as the spirit of the living God is poured out upon you through His word that you will respond in kind by pouring into someone else through words of salvation, love, encouragement, and/or healing so that they too will be able to emerge beautiful – a new creation before Him. I pray this prayer believing now that it has been answered in none other than the matchless name of our Lord and Savior, Jesus Christ. To God be all glory, and honor, and praise, Alleluia!

Quick Trips

Psalm 119: 11, 16, 105	Proverbs 2:1-5
Proverbs 30:5	Isaiah 55:11
Matthew 24:35	Romans 10:8
James 1:21	

Notes

For we are God's fellow workers; you are God's field, God's building.

(1 Corinthians 3:9)

Women of God

A very eclectic and passionate writer, Maya Angelou has authored a myriad of poems. Word after word, she weaves beautiful imagery of fantastical images in which many of us see our lives reflected. Amongst her writings are poems of relationship, love, spirituality, and inspiration. Included in some of her most famous pieces, among others; are, *Life Doesn't Frighten Me, And Still I Rise, On the Pulse of Morning,* and *Phenomenal Woman.*

In Phenomenal Woman, Maya explains the reasons why, despite her larger than fashion model's size, she can attract and sustain a man's attention. Listing the size and sway of her hips, the arch of her back, and the fire in her eyes as enticement; she paints a picture of confidence, elegance, and boldness. As the poem continues, she lists area by area through which her seduction is portrayed.

A beautifully crafted piece of art, many women have opted to buy into it. Consequently, Maya's claim to fame has resulted in many women electing to adopt Phenomenal Woman as their personal mantra ultimately forsaking all else for the ultimate pursuit of beauty in the physical realm as opposed to spiritual beauty. In turn, women of all shapes and sizes use this fleeting description as a vehicle through which they validate and ultimately glean approval from their peers and/or members of the opposite sex. In the eyes of God however women are called to be more than their looks, more than objects of a man's attraction. Evidenced throughout the Bible, God has used women not only to fulfill His prophecy but to bring redemption to His people.

One such of these women was Deborah. A judge in her time God's calling and anointing upon her life helped her to defeat the Canaanites, lead the Israelites out of idolatry, as well as help remind them of the covenant they had with God. (Judges 4 -5)

Another such example is Esther. Although she was beautiful, her anointing for obedience as well as intercessory prayer was so effective that she was able to expose the plans of the wicked Haman and in turn vindicate her people. (Esther 1 – 10)

Last to be mentioned, but not the least of them, was Abigail. Generous, wise, and smart, God's anointing on her made her one through which peacemaking tactics were employed to help divert a bloody as well needless battle. (1 Samuel 25: 2-42)

Summarized above were three women whose actions were necessary for the revelation and enactment of God's plan. Although they were each beautiful in their own right, none of them allowed their beauty to hinder the call God had on their lives. As Christian women we should not be so consumed with our physical appearance so much so that it causes us to lose sight of God's plan for our lives. Rather, we should constantly be in search of the part God would have us play in the plan to ultimately bring to fruition His kingdom here on earth.

It is my prayer for each of you today that your beauty does not hinder you from seeking God's desire for your life. In seeking His will, I pray that He will reveal to you your area of expertise as well as the area of action in which He would have you operate. Lastly, it is my prayer that you will make every attempt to seek out like women so that in agreement God will be able to strengthen you all as you sharpen each other for His glory. I pray this prayer believing now that it has been answered in none other than the matchless name of our Lord and Savior, Jesus Christ. To God be all glory, and honor, and praise, Alleluia!

Quick Trips

Proverbs 9:13-18	Proverbs 11:16
Proverbs 12:14	Proverbs 14:1
Proverbs 19:13-14	Proverbs 23:27
Proverbs 27:15-16	Proverbs 31:10-31

Chapter Four: Deliverance

There is a way which seems right to a man, but its end is the way of death.

(Proverbs 16:25, NASB)

About Face!

      Although I was able to complete an intense hour and a half of aerobics during my gym rat days, the art of long distance running always seemed to have eluded me. Whether it was because of poor breathing habits, my short stride, or the *'old faithful'* recurring stitch in my side after step nine; running was something on which I was just never able to get a grip. Consequently, I often marveled at those who made the act look like such an easy task and, in an effort to supplement my inability; I often found myself watching marathons on TV just to get a glimpse of the perfect form, the ideal stride. Conversely, it might amaze you to know that such was not the case in the spirit. Utilizing Forest Gump's catalyst for action, my escape mantra from the Lord became, "Run, Danie, run!"

      An expert marathoner in the spirit, I ran from the Lord for a period of thirty five years. Ironically, all the hindrances that stood in my way in the physical realm never showed themselves adversaries in the realm of the spirit. As such; my systems check always went something like this: "Breathing habits?" "Check!" "Graceful stride?" "Check!" "Stitch?" "None!" In excellent form, I ran farther and farther away from the call God had placed on my life thinking that if I ran far enough away He would finally give up and leave me alone. Fortunately for me, and because He already knew the plans He had for me, though I ran; He never gave up.

Like Jonah, (Jonah 1 – 4) it seemed as though the farther away I got from Him the more He reminded me of my calling. The farther out of His will I ran, the more He chastised. The longer I disregarded his directives, the more grace He extended. Finally, between the proverbial *rock and a hard place* and with nowhere else to turn I hearkened to His call, surrendered to His will, and ran no more. Since then, I have witnessed firsthand the glory of God in my life and I thank Him every day for never forsaking me.

In two short years (2006 – 2008), He has groomed and released me in my purpose, supernaturally provided for my children and I, created in me a clean heart, and called my children unto Him. He has forgiven me of my sins allowing me to walk in shame and guilt no longer, and has made way a path of righteousness for me to follow. In short, because I stopped running away from and chose to surrender to Him instead, He was able to complete a quick work in me and all to His glory. Alleluia!

As such, I am proud to say that I no longer run from my heavenly Father. As a matter of fact, I fervently now run towards Him, embracing His will entirely. In other words, I am now a marathon runner for my Lord seeking solace in Him as I run full speed ahead into His outstretched arms vowing that He will never have to chase me again! My Brothers and Sisters are you marathon runners for our Lord and Savior Jesus Christ or, like Jonah; are you running away from God's call and purpose on your life?

It is my prayer for each of you today that you be reminded of God's purpose for your life. I pray if there be any of you who fear the call God has placed upon your life that there be an immediate conviction in your spirit. I pray that with that conviction you may be able to repent of running from and instead turn back to Him in seeking His desires for your life. Lastly, I pray that God will make your way straight as you submit to His call. I pray this prayer believing now that it has been answered in none other than the matchless name of our Lord and Savior, Jesus Christ. To God be all glory, and honor, and praise, Alleluia!

Quick Trips

Psalms 27:1	Psalms 23:3
Psalms 37:4, 7, 23	Psalms 18:10

Proverbs 1:33	Proverbs 14:12
Isaiah 48:17	Isaiah 58:11
Romans 8:31-32	Romans 8:28
James 4:6-7	Proverbs 3:5-6

Notes

Just as Sodom and Gomorrah and the cities around them,
since they in the same way as these indulged in gross immorality
and went after strange flesh,
are exhibited as an example in undergoing the punishment of
eternal fire.
(Jude: 7, NASB)

Deliverance from Immorality

Everywhere we look, we are inundated with images of sexuality, images used to stir the spirit of lust within us. Through the use of billboards, television shows and advertisements, as well as magazines – just to name a few – sexuality, whether we like it or not; has become a major vehicle through which our attention is captivated.

If that were not enough, the use of sexuality has even made its way into some children's programming as a means to entice our young children into the world. Via the use of seductive clothing and/or make up, implicit sexual humor, as well as the embedding of adult situations into said programs, i.e. dating, jealousy in relationships, and relational betrayals; children are being exposed to the world of sexuality at an earlier age. In response to this, and as opposed to reacting according to the Word of God; some teach their children safe sex practices, purchase contraceptives, and/or encourage them to 'sow their wild oats' prior to getting married and settling down. What is worst, sometimes children do not even have to look farther than their parents' own lifestyles to identify with or be introduced to the spirit of lust and all that it entails as adulterous affairs, loose sexual practices, sex outside of God's design of marriage, and pornography.

On this, the Word is very clear.

> Or do you not know that the unrighteous will not inherit the kingdom of God? Do not be deceived; neither **fornicators**, nor idolaters, nor **adulterers**, nor **effeminate**, nor **homosexuals**, nor thieves, nor the covetous, nor drunkards, nor revilers, nor swindlers, will inherit the kingdom of God. (1 Corinthians 6:9-10, NASB)

However, although it is written, many fall prey and succumb to the temptation of the flesh. I did. Were it not for the grace of God, and the repentance of my sin, as well as the study of His most sacred teachings, I too would still be counted amongst those listed in the above referenced Scripture. As such it is important to note that, although no sin is weighed heavily than the other, immorality is the only sin we perpetrate, "against our own bodies." (1 Corinthians 6:18) One for which we will be separated from our Father.

Why then would any one – having availed themselves to the Word - knowingly choose to defile the temple of the living God? 1 Corinthians 6:9-10 tells us that not only have we been bought for a price, but that through that purchase our bodies are no longer our own, but rather that of the living God. Why then my Brothers and Sisters would we knowingly use our bodies for anything less than what they have been designed - to bring glory as a living sacrifice unto the most high God?

It is my prayer for each of you today that you will be consumed with the living fire of the most High as he burns away any fleshly desires you may have that are contrary to His teachings. I pray now, standing on the promise of Matthew 16:19 that the spirit of the flesh (lust) will be cast out of you in the name of Jesus Christ. I pray that in its place you will be renewed with the desire to cleanse and maintain your temple according to His commandments. I pray all guilt and shame removed from you as you repent of your sins. As your house has now been cleansed, I pray that our Lord and Savior, Jesus Christ will give you the strength to withstand any further temptation; that in your weakness, His strength will be made whole. Lastly, I pray that as you are made stronger in your new found freedom that the ministry will be furthered through you as you stand up and proclaim the teachings of our Lord. I pray this prayer believing now that it has been answered in none other than the matchless name of our Lord and Savior, Jesus Christ. To God be all glory, and honor, and praise, Alleluia!

Quick Trips

Leviticus 18:22-24	Leviticus 20: 10, 13, 15-16
Matthew 5:28	Deuteronomy 22:25-27
Mark 10:19	Colossians 3:5
2 Timothy 3:1-3	Ephesians 5:3-12

Notes

Indeed, the very hairs of your head are all numbered. Do not fear; you are more valuable than many sparrows.

(Luke 12:7, NASB)

Fear Not

The world would point to the failing economy as the reason for the recent increase in crime. However those in the spirit would argue that "we battle not against flesh and blood, but against… spiritual forces of wickedness…" Nonetheless, it is easy to see how either one of these arguments could perpetuate fear amongst the masses. Let me expound…

This past Saturday, I attended a taser party. Set into place by my subdivision's home owner's association, but presented by one of Atlanta's leading names in self defense products, the function was indeed an eye opener to the various levels of crime associated within the city and its adjacent areas. During the presentation, several incidents of rape; carjacking; and home invasions were described as a preface to the sales pitch. Disclosed to sales persons by various clients or either as a result of paging through local police blotters the plying of these unfortunate incidents were rendered for the sole purpose of raising the fear factor in the room. As a logical seg-way, the presenters used the above mentioned crimes as their rationale as to why we should not be without protection.

As I watched in amazement at the raw power released from the non-lethal weapons, I too began to think about purchasing one to secure myself and my family from the many hideous possibilities mentioned above. At the very least, I even considered purchasing a secret safe in which to secure our personal belongings. But, as I listened attentively to the Voice within – His voice – it became very clear that self protection was not necessary as my family, my possessions, and my home had already been covered. Still, as the spirit of the living God within me wrestled with the voice of the world it became even more apparent that the driving force behind the success of Saturday's weapons sales – the money making entity of the business – was indeed the spirit of fear.

As defined by the Cambridge online Dictionary fear is *an unpleasant emotion or thought that you have when you are frightened or worried by something dangerous, painful or bad that is happening or might happen*. Defined both in the present and future tense, fear then is something that can cause one to make decisions not based upon fact, or evidence; but rather based upon suspicion.

Please note however, as written in 2 Timothy 1:7,

> "God hath not given us the spirit of fear; but of power, and of love, and of a sound mind. (NASB)

As such, the behavior and/or life of a Christian should not be based upon the suspicion of what could happen next, but rather upon the knowledge that God has warned us to stand firm in the power of a sound mind. Accordingly so and evidenced both in the Old and New Testaments, the context in which the command "Fear not," is given never changes. Who are we then to doubt the Living word of God?

My Brothers and Sisters, of what are you afraid? In what realm are you being held captive? Are you walking gingerly according to the whim of the spirit of fear or are you walking boldly in the promises of God making a mental note and spiritual action to fear not?

My prayer for each of you today is simply this: Standing on the promise of Matthew 16:19 I loose now the spirit of fear from upon you in the name of Jesus Christ our Savior and bind in its place an out pouring of confidence in our God. I decree and declare now that you have been delivered from the spirit fear as Jesus is the only name we know. I pray this prayer believing now that it has been answered in none other than the matchless name of our Lord and Savior, Jesus Christ. To God be all glory, and honor, and praise, Alleluia!

Quick Trips

Genesis 15:1	Deuteronomy 1:21
Joshua 8:1	1 Chronicles 28:20
Jeremiah 46:27	John 14:27
Isaiah 26:3	Psalm 119:65
Psalm 27:1	

Notes

___
___
___
___
___
___
___
___
___
___
___
___
___
___

"I brought you into the fruitful land to eat its fruit and its good things but you came and defiled My land, and My inheritance you made an abomination."

(Jeremiah 2:7, NASB)

Guises of the Enemy

Before I was saved, I delighted daily in reading my horoscope to the point where not only would I purchase the newspaper to see what my future held, I would also surf the internet to see if both forms of media were in agreement. Similarly, I was a huge fan of chained emails that promised the granting of a wish if forwarded, or worse the befalling of a curse if not. However, although there was a diminutive amount of generic hits on the horoscope predictions, there was an exponential amount of misses. Further and as expected, none of the wishes I ever made on a chain e-mail has been granted. This is so for two reasons.

First, the desire to seek knowledge or wisdom through any realm other than through God is an abomination unto Him. Deuteronomy 18:9-12 states,

> "When thou art come into the land which the Lord thy God giveth thee, thou shalt not learn to do after the abominations of those nations. There shall not be found among you any one that maketh his son or his daughter to pass through the fire, or that useth divination, or an observer of times, or an enchanter, or a witch, or a charmer, or a consulter with familiar spirits, or a wizard, or a necromancer. For all that do these things are an abomination unto the LORD: and because of these abominations the LORD thy God doth drive them out from before thee." (KJV)

Another version, The Message states,

> When you enter the land that GOD, your God, is giving you, don't take on the abominable ways of life of the nations there. Don't you dare sacrifice your son or daughter in the fire. Don't practice divination, sorcery, fortune telling, witchery, casting spells, holding séances, or channeling with the dead. People who do these things are an abomination to GOD. It's because of just such abominable practices that GOD, your God, is driving these nations out before you.

As defined by the Cambridge Online Dictionary, divination is the *skill or act of saying what will happen in the future or discovering something that is unknown or secret by magical methods.* Also considered as casting a spell, a directive to forward a message to unsuspecting parties so as not to incur a curse upon one's self is also frowned upon by our Lord. In essence, these two acts, though different breeds; are both in direct abomination to

God, grounds for being driven away from Him. Is this not what the enemy wants?

The second reason one should not resort to the reliance of horoscopes to get a glimpse into the future, or wanting wishes granted in exchange for forwarding messages is that these acts force us to place our trust in and cleave to something other than God and His perfect will for our lives. God chastised the Israelites for their overwhelming fear of the Amorites saying,

> "The Lord your God who goes before you will Himself fight on your behalf just as He did for you in Egypt before your eyes, and in the wilderness where you saw how the LORD your God carried you, just as a man carries his son, in all the way which you have walked until you came to this place. But for all this, you did not trust the LORD your God, who goes before you on your way, to seek out a place for you to encamp, in fire by night and cloud by day, to show you the way in which you should go. (Deuteronomy 1:30-33) (NASB)

Applicable too in this sense, the Lord would have us cling to the belief that He is in front of us making our path straight as well as free from incident. In return, we would simply have to trust in Him for our future is all in His hands. Consequently, if we were not to heed His warning in these matters and opt to still seek guidance from the hand of the enemy, we will ultimately fast track ourselves to being cut off from God and our promised land in pretty much the same way the Israelites were. (Deuteronomy 1:34-35) (NASB)

Lastly, it would be prudent to note that nothing is ever accomplished without the help of the Holy Spirit. Evidenced in Zechariah 4:6 (NASB), the angel tells the prophet;

> "This is the word of the LORD to Zerubbabel saying, not by might nor by power, but by My Spirit,' says the LORD of hosts."

In short, no amount of witchcraft, divination, and/or spell casting will get you into the presence of God. Quite the contrary, you will be banished from Him completely and not be able to walk into your promised land lest you cease and repent of your ways.

It is my prayer for each of you today that whether through deliberate action or ignorance that you cease and desist from any act the Lord deems abominable. I pray now standing on the promise of Matthew 16:19 that the spirit of divination be loosed from you in the name of Jesus Christ, and in its place the binding of a renewed sense of faith and trust in the Lord. I pray that once your house is in order concerning these things, that He will be swift to reestablish you to His promises for your life. Lastly, I pray that as this message blesses you that you will see fit to pass on the knowledge of the Lord so that no more of His sheep will be caused to suffer. I pray this prayer believing now that it has been answered in none other than the matchless name of our Lord and

Savior, Jesus Christ. To God be all glory, and honor, and praise, Alleluia!

Quick Trips

1 Peter 5:8	Colossians 2:15
John 10:10	John 14:30
Ephesians 6:12	Ephesians 4:27
Philippians 4:8	James 1:15

Notes

For this cause we also, since the day we heard it, do not cease to pray for you, and to desire that ye might be filled with the knowledge of his will in all wisdom and spiritual understanding; That ye might walk worthy of the Lord unto all pleasing, being fruitful in every good work, and increasing in the knowledge of God; Strengthened with all might, according to his glorious power, unto all patience and longsuffering with joyfulness;
(Colossians 1:9-11)

In Him, This Too Shall Pass!

I was led to 1 Corinthians 10: 1- 13 this morning as an encouragement to God's people. Please heed the promise. The passage reads:

> For I do not want you to be unaware, brethren that our fathers were all under the cloud and all passed through the sea; and all were baptized into Moses in the cloud and in the sea; and all ate the same spiritual food; and all drank the same spiritual drink, for they were drinking from a spiritual rock which followed them; and the rock was Christ.

Nevertheless, with most of them God was not well-pleased; for they were laid low in the wilderness. Now these things happened as examples for us, so that we would not crave evil things as they also craved. Do not be idolaters, as some of them were; as it is written, "THE PEOPLE SAT DOWN TO EAT AND DRINK, AND STOOD UP TO PLAY." Nor let us act immorally, as some of them did, and twenty-three thousand fell in one day. Nor let us try the Lord, as some of them did, and were destroyed by the serpents. Nor grumble, as some of them did, and were destroyed by the destroyer. Now these things happened to them as an example, and they were written for our instruction, upon whom the ends of the ages have come. Therefore let him who thinks he stands take heed that he does not fall.

No temptation has overtaken you but such as is common to man; and God is faithful, who will not allow you to be tempted beyond what you are able, but with the temptation will provide the way of escape also, so that you will be able to endure it. *(*New American Standard Bible) *(Author's emphasis)*

Although the caption above admonishes us to, *Avoid Israel's Mistakes* – which we would be remiss not to heed - today's focus is found in verse thirteen where it is explained that God will (1) never give us more than we can bear, and (2) always provide a way out for us. Alleluia!

It is my prayer for each of you today that you will find solace in knowing that the Lord is bigger than any circumstance or situation that you may be going through. I pray that in addition to knowing Him as your provider, healer, way-maker, etc; that you will also recognize Him as the God of Hosts who encompasses all things great and small. As such, it is my prayer that you **will** not fall victim to the guises and/or vices of this world. In the name of Jesus Christ, I decree that the enemy's influence over you is no more!

    I declare endurance, peace, faith and resilience upon you now so that you will be able to stand firm on the promise that joy does indeed come in the morning. Further, it is my prayer that despite your circumstance, you will lift up your voice in praise, thanksgiving, and adoration to the most high God crying out to Him from the depths of your soul. Lastly, as your praise is made acceptable unto Him, it is my prayer that He will inhabit your praise. I pray this prayer believing now that it has been answered in none other than the matchless name of our Lord and Savior, Jesus Christ. To God be all glory, and honor, and praise, Alleluia!

Quick Trips

1 Timothy 6:12	2 Timothy 4:7
2 Samuel 22:3-4	1 John 5:4-5
1 Corinthians 15:57	2 Corinthians 2:14
Isaiah 54:17	Luke 10:19

You are from God, little children, and have overcome them; because greater is He who is in you than he who is in the world. (1 John 4:4, NASB)

Real Life Reality Game Show

      Browsing through the channels one can stumble upon any given number of reality shows on any given night. There has been an influx of reality shows on television throughout the years. Specifically so, the listing of available reality television includes, however is not limited to; shows that encourage people to lose weight, or be the best cook they can be; shows that seek to find the next big, new talent in dance and/or song; as well as shows that assist some in finding 'true' love.

      Despite the fact that some of these shows are riddled with divisiveness, backstabbing, lies, and the formation of allies for the sole purpose of overtaking one's fellow man we make it our business to tune in, nonetheless. Unfortunately, it is this type of discord that fuels our interest, the type of discord amongst the brethren God hates (Proverbs 6:19), that causes us to tune in on a weekly basis. However, what many of us do not realize is that browsing through the channels is not necessary for the viewing of a prime time reality show. We function within one every day.

Aptly entitled, *Lie to You* the adversary has devised a reality game show in which there are many contestants who – some unawares – are playing for the loss of their souls to eternal damnation. Playing the game along the rules/lies of (1) you are unworthy of God's unconditional love; (2) your transgressions are unforgivable; (3) you have time – party on; (4) you will never amount to anything; and/or (5) there is no deliverance from your past hurts, addictions, vices, and/or worldly pleasures, many fall victim to the belief that they are stuck in a vicious, unending cycle. As a result of this deceit, many end up throwing caution to the wind ultimately jeopardizing their chances of everlasting life.

One of the reasons one might say the enemy attacks is to strategically plot to disqualify those who, if put to use on the winning side, would threaten and thereby raise a raucous in his plans. Is that not the way it is done on televised reality shows? Are not the most threatening contestants the ones with the bull's eye on their backs? Why then would it be any different in the realm of spiritual warfare?

As such, if you find yourself a victim of the enemy's repeated attacks it would behoove you to ask yourself, "What threat would I be to the enemy if I were counted as one of the arrows (Psalm 127:4) in the hands of the Lord? What is it about you my Brothers and Sisters that intimidate the enemy? Further, what God given talents have you not yet activated for the kingdom that once in place could yield a major blow to the enemy's plot?

It is my prayer for each of you this afternoon, that you seek the Lord to reveal to you your purpose in His kingdom. I pray that He makes clear the plans that He has already ordained for you prior to your birth (Jeremiah 1:5) (Jeremiah 29:11-14). Lastly, I pray that once you have gained the heavenly insight into the role you are to play in the kingdom that you will act in swift obedience responding only to the voice of the Lord. (John 5:19) I pray this prayer believing now that it has been answered in none other than the matchless name of our Lord and Savior, Jesus Christ. To God be all glory, and honor, and praise, Alleluia!

Quick Trips

Isaiah 55:10-12	Matthew 25:14-28
1 Corinthians 12:4, 7-11	1 Corinthians 7:7
1 Corinthians 14:12	Romans 11:29
Romans 12:6-8	Peter 4:10

Blessed be the God and Father of our Lord Jesus Christ,
Who has blessed us with every spiritual blessing in the heavenly places in Christ,
just as He chose us in Him before the foundation of the world, that we would be holy and blameless before Him
(Ephesians 1:3-4, NASB)

Sanctified, Whole, and Blameless

One Sunday, I spent the better part of the evening doubled over in pain. Just a few minutes earlier, I had prayed and asked the Lord to break a soul tie. In an instant, my stomach turned and my body was riddled with pain. The discomfort was so intense my children did not leave my side for the rest of the night nor the following day. Nothing I did seemed to ease the pain. Finally at my wits end; I pondered if what I had prayed for in the spirit could also have been manifesting itself in the physical. As the Lord would have it, He led me to 1 Thessalonians 5:23-24 which states,

> "And the very God of peace sanctify you wholly; and I pray God your

> whole spirit and soul and body be preserved blameless unto the coming of our Lord Jesus Christ. Faithful is he that calleth you, who also will do it." (KJV)

In receiving my answer, it was evident that we were created in three parts –spirits, souls, and bodies.

As such, in asking Him to break a soul tie in my spirit He also had to do so in my soul and in my body in an attempt to *"preserve me blameless"* before Him. According to the scripture, not only was I being made whole and sanctified in anticipation of the coming of our Lord, but He was also presenting Himself faithful to what I had asked Him to do. I had indeed been delivered! Long story short, despite the discomfort I endured in the physical, it was definitely worth the experience to be made whole and made blameless before God.

What soul ties do you need to have broken so that you too can stand blameless before Him? It is my prayer for each of you today that you beseech the Lord in breaking any soul ties that may hinder you from standing blameless before Him. I pray that as the ties are broken, you will be able to release any grudges and/or bitterness still held against the person to whom you are tied. Lastly, I pray that the presence of the Lord will comfort and fill any voids that are left so that you will be made whole in spirit, soul, and body unto Him. I pray this prayer believing now that it has been answered in none other than the matchless name of our

Lord and Savior, Jesus Christ. To God be all glory, and honor, and praise, Alleluia!

Quick Trips

Philippians 1:9-10   Philippians 2:15
1 Thessalonians 2:10   Revelation 14:4-5
1 Thessalonians 5:23   Jude 24
1 Corinthians 1:8   1 Timothy 6:14
Hebrews 4:14-16   Luke 1:6
    Colossians 1:22-23
    1 Thessalonians 3:12:13

Notes

_____
_____
_____
_____   _____
_____
_____
_____
_____   _____

"Yet they did not obey or incline their ear,
but walked in their own counsels and in the stubbornness of
their evil heart,
and went backward and not forward.
(Jeremiah 7:24, NASB)

Stubbornness or Obedience: Punishment or Reward?

The act of stubbornness or rebellion has always been attributed to that of a mule. For some, being "Stubborn as a mule" is a daily reminder of their character. For many this character trait may be innate, for others a choice. Nonetheless, no matter the distinction; both are in direct violation of God's Word and, as evidenced in 1 Samuel 15:23; rebellion is akin to witchcraft.

"For rebellion is as the sin of divination, and insubordination is as iniquity and idolatry, because you have rejected the word of the LORD, He has also rejected you from being king." (NASB)

Based on its categorization, stubbornness is a trait not applauded by our Lord. In fact, one can find themselves quickly out of the grace of God for his/her stubbornness.

Exhibited in many ways, the ramifications of stubbornness are present in many a workplace, many a relationship. A refusal to yield to leadership, stubbornness exhibits itself in different ways. For example, acting against those in authority; acting out against rules; or even refusing to conform to the standard and acceptable mode of behavior are all counted as stubbornness. (Cambridge Online Dictionary)

Applied to the workplace, stubbornness can be the refusal to accept the decision of one's supervisor during his/her normal and expected course of duty, or; in refusing to conform to the company's standards of decorum and professional behavior. Applied in relationships, rebellion can be experienced as one partner blatantly disregards the other. Moreover, practicing stubbornness defiles relationships and allows for resentment and hurt to attack the injured party while breeding a false sense of self love and pride in the offender.

A dangerous attribute to uphold on so many levels, the reward of stubbornness is grim. Found in Psalms 10:4 David establishes that which the stubborn person is capable. He also asks of the Lord to silence them in death.

Let their lying lips be silenced, for with pride and contempt they speak arrogantly against the righteous. (NASB)

Although David's request may seem harsh, think for a moment about your interactions with a stubborn person. Do they not make things more difficult than they should be? Does not their refusal to adhere to those in charge or their refusal to support the established operating rules of an organization not bring chaos and resentment into the mix? Does not their constant complaining to have it done their way or, rather their never-ending manipulation of the system and the people around them undermine the cohesiveness of all involved? Indeed it would. Stubbornness, my friends; is not of God. Though prayed against by David, it is ultimately punishable by the Most High.

When the Lord gave His rewards and punishments for disobedience to the Israelites, He said unto them,

"If after all this you will not listen to me, I will punish you for your sins seven times over. I will break down your stubborn pride and make the sky above you like iron and the ground beneath you like bronze. Your strength will be spent in vain, because your soil will not yield its crops, nor will the trees of the land yield their fruit." (Leviticus 26:18-20, NASB)

Likewise, the Lord admonished the stubborn saying,

"But because of your stubbornness and unrepentant heart you are storing up wrath for yourself in the day of wrath and revelation of the righteous judgment of God, who will render to each person according to his deeds: to those who by perseverance in doing good seek for glory and honor and immortality, eternal life; but to those who are selfishly ambitious and do not obey the truth, but obey unrighteousness, wrath and indignation." (Romans 2:5-8, NASB)

As such my Brothers and Sisters, what judgment would you rather face, a judgment in which you are separated eternally from Him; or a judgment in which you will be received with open arms for your humility and obedience?

It is my prayer for you today that if there be any stubbornness within you that it be removed. Standing on God's promise of Matthew 16:19, I loose off you the spirit of haughtiness in the name of Jesus Christ our Savior, and bind in its place the heart of a servant whose desire it is to serve at all times. I pray that as you assume the posture of humility that you adhere to His Word in full obedience of His commands. I pray that as you submit to His leading that He will bless you as He prescribed in Deuteronomy 28:1-14 for your obedience. I pray this prayer believing now that it has been answered in none other than the matchless name of our Lord and Savior, Jesus Christ. To God be all glory, and honor, and praise, Alleluia!

Quick Trips

Proverbs 3:34	Proverbs 3:7
Proverbs 21:4	Proverbs 15:33
Romans 12:3	2 Chronicles 7:14
James 4:10	Galatians 6:3-4
Isaiah 66:2	Ephesians 2:9
Habakkuk 2:4	1 Peter 5:5-6

Notes

For we are His workmanship, created in Christ Jesus for good works, which God prepared beforehand so that we would walk in them.

(Ephesians 2:10, NASB)

The Pinnacle of the Mountain

Like *The Little Train that Could*, we often think that we can scale to the tops of life's mountains under our own steam and virtue for our own validation. It is not until we try and try again that the frustration settles into our bones and we ask ourselves why nothing we do seems to work.

As a young girl, I often remember my father remarking in frustration, "Just as soon as you are about to get to the pinnacle of the mountain, something always seems to pull you back down!" Too young then to understand what it meant, I never really gave the phrase much thought. However as I grew, this phrase would evolve to find itself a part of my life as I quipped in aggravation about many a stumbling block I encountered throughout the years.

For example, although I worked hard and prided myself on my studies; my four year Bachelor of Arts degree actually turned into a five year stint. If that was not discouraging enough, when I finally graduated with the degree I was not employed until two years later. Further, after beginning my career in education and gaining a small level of fame, I still was not able to make the impact of which I had always dreamed. Most recently, even though my relocation to Georgia was made in good conscious and intentions, things did not begin to 'happen' for me in the order that I expected them to. Relatively enough, just as my father posited all those many years ago; not being able to get to the crest of the mountain had finally made itself relevant to and evident in my life.

However although my frustrations were based upon the emotion of disappointment, they were also rooted in the ultimate emotion of pride. You see, it was not until my walk with Christ did I come to realize that despite all my grandiose ideas, lofty goals, and selfish agendas that my motivations were not pure. For the most part, they were selfish and based on external drive as opposed to intrinsic satisfaction. They were staged for the good of Danielle as opposed to for the good of the people to whom the services were intended. Finally, my hidden agenda was such that in trying to complete all the goals I had set, the ultimate reason was for my own uplifting and prominence. To say the least, though well intentioned, my actions were not based in humility.

Proverbs 16: 19 clearly states,

> "Better it is to be of a humble spirit with the lowly, than to divide the spoil with the proud." (NASB)

Likewise Proverbs 29: 23 states,

> "A man's pride shall bring him low: but honor shall uphold the humble in spirit." (NASB)

In similar fashion Matthew 23:12 says,

> "And whosoever shall exalt himself shall be abased; and he that shall humble himself shall be exalted. (NASB)

Additionally James 4:10 states,

> "Humble yourselves in the sight of the Lord, and he shall lift you up." (NASB)

And lastly, my personal favorite; I Peter 5: 5 – 7 states,

> "Humble yourselves therefore under the mighty hand of God, that he may exalt you in due time." (NASB)

By the listing of these five scriptures, it is evident that the selfish, self centered person will not be exalted or uplifted in God's eyes.

Rather than watch us run to ruin, is it then plausible to believe that God could throw a monkey wrench into our plans if He deemed us getting too big for our britches? Is if fathomable to think that God in His infinite wisdom could cause us to suffer setbacks in an attempt to continue to mold us in preparation for our exaltation in Him all the while drawing us near? Could it be then that His plan for the crest of the mountain we so desperately strive to get to on our own is reserved for those whom He alone places there?

In an attempt to answer that question, now that I look back on all those setbacks with my spiritual eyes I can see the hand of God on 99.9% of them. It is evident that as He molded me throughout my many disappointments and setbacks it was all to His glory. In the process, I gleaned exactly what it was that He set out for me to receive. Long story short, because I never got to the pinnacle of the mountain on my own, I am all the better for it in Him. Finally, it was not until I totally humbled myself to Him and gave Him total control of my life, did I reap the benefit of my exaltation manifested through His release of my gifting in service to His people.

In closing I ask you, how have you been trying to get to the pinnacle of the mountain? Has it been on your own under your own steam like *The Little Train Who Could*, or by the Father's exaltation? If on your own, what area of your life have you not submitted to the Holy Spirit that is hindering you from getting there? Or could it be the hand of God on your life saving you from the perils of pride?

Whatever the reason, it is my prayer today that you are able to shed any prior instances of frustrations that you have had in being swept from the pinnacle of the mountain just as you thought you had arrived. In releasing those frustrations, I pray that you would then fully surrender your life to God so that His word may be a lamp unto your feet and a light unto your path (Psalm 119:105.) I pray a releasing of a renewed confidence in Him so that you will be able to hear His voice and be obedient to His will. It is my prayer today that in your obedience to honor Him in humility that you will reap exaltation through Him at the appointed time. I pray this prayer believing now that it has been answered in none other than the matchless name of our Lord and Savior, Jesus Christ. To God be all glory, and honor, and praise, Alleluia!

Quick Trips

Habakkuk 2:3   Acts 1:7
1 Thessalonians 2:6   Titus 1:3

Notes

For though we walk in the flesh, we do not war after the flesh: (For the weapons of our warfare are not carnal, but mighty through God to the pulling down of strong holds;) Casting down imaginations, and every high thing that exalteth itself against the knowledge of God, and bringing into captivity every thought to the obedience of Christ; And having in a readiness to revenge all disobedience, when your obedience is fulfilled.

(2 Corinthians 10:3-6, KJV)

Under Attack

After spending the majority of yesterday morning transporting my children to various doctors' appointments we all returned tired enough to warrant an afternoon nap. In fact we were so tired that even after dinner we found ourselves the victim of our television's attention as opposed to vice versa. Realizing that we were not able to fight the good fight of consciousness any longer we raised the white flag of surrender and headed for our beds, each to our individual dream worlds.

Unfortunately for me however; and as a result of the tiredness that stemmed from the business of the day, my sleep was restless; my dreams awful. In one dream, I was witness to a murder I had tried to cover up; in another, I was unsuccessfully interceding for someone who had eventually lost their lives; and lastly in yet another dream, I had succumbed to and enjoyed the temptation of my flesh.

Attacked in the three closely guarded areas of my walk with Christ, I awoke the next morning, not as rested as I should have been. Confused with the complexity of my dreams, I pondered in silent prayer and reflection as I immediately began to search my heart asking the Lord to cleanse me of any thoughts, actions, and/or words that could have caused me to dream in the manner which I did the night before. As I prayed, the Holy Spirit led me to several truths.

First, I was reminded that, "the devil prowls around like a roaring lion, seeking someone to devour." (1 Peter 5:8, NASB) I was also reminded that if I, "Submit therefore to God and resist the devil, he will flee from me." (James 4:7, NASB) With those two impartations, it became quite obvious that (1) I had been in the midst of spiritual warfare the night before; and (2) that though I battled not in the flesh, the presence of the Holy Spirit was indeed warring right along with me while I slept.

Accordingly so, it would be prudent to mention that the enemy is indeed coy and uses many vehicles through which he either tempts us or tries to deliver us into sin. Although it is said that, "He is like a roaring lion seeking whom he may devour," his attacks on our righteousness are at times disguised in either dreams, as our own voice, intellect, and/or emotions. Moreover, his temptations can either overwhelm us or they can be as subtle as a misguided thought rooted not within the principles God.

For this reason, Ephesians 6:12 warns,

> "For we wrestle not against flesh and blood, but against principalities, against powers, against the rulers of the darkness of this world, against spiritual wickedness in high places."

Continuing in Ephesians 6:13-18; Paul gives us a list of the spiritual armor necessary for protection against the enemy's attacks.

> "Wherefore take unto you the whole armor of God that ye may be able to withstand in the evil day, and having done all, to stand. Stand therefore, having your loins girt about with truth, and having on the breastplate of righteousness; and your feet shod with the preparation of the gospel of peace; above all, taking the shield of faith, wherewith ye shall be able to quench all the fiery darts of the wicked. And take the helmet of salvation, and the sword of the Spirit, which is the word of God: praying always with all prayer and supplication in the Spirit, and watching thereunto with all perseverance and supplication for all saints;" (KJV)

My Brothers and Sisters are you fully clothed in the armor of the Lord? Or, have you left areas of your spirit, soul, and/or body susceptible to attacks from the enemy?

It is my prayer for each of you today that you put on the whole armor of God thus girding yourself with the protection needed to defeat the enemy in all his ways. It is my prayer that you will be able to discern the many ways in which the enemy will come against you so that you may be wise to his many tricks. Lastly, I pray that the shelter of the Lord may prove an additional layer of protection upon you as you continue to walk with and trust in Him as He creates within you a clean heart. I pray this prayer believing now that it has been answered in none other than the matchless name of our Lord and Savior, Jesus Christ. To God be all glory, and honor, and praise, Alleluia!

Quick Trips

Genesis 3:1	Genesis 3:4
Matthew 4:3, 6	John 8:44
Isaiah 54:17	Malachi 4:3
Luke 10:19	1 John 4:4

Notes

> For our struggle is not against flesh and blood, but against the rulers, against the powers, against the world forces of this darkness, against the spiritual forces of wickedness in the heavenly places.
>
> (Ephesians 6:12, NASB)

Warfare

The body of Christ is being attacked more than ever before in instances that many equate to the everyday functions of life - i.e. children acting out, marriages failing, jobs being lost, happiness and contentment waning, lost wages, illness, addictions, stubbornness, uncooperativeness, persecution, etc. As such many have lost their faith in Him or worse have questioned His sovereignty. As a result, the enemy is gaining ground as God's people turn away in an effort to solve problems on their own as opposed to standing on His promises - the end result of which is too many of God's children, our brothers and sisters, being led astray and lost to this world.

Accordingly so and in obedience to the leading of the Holy Spirit, this morning's message is a call to arms. Just as the Israelites praised down in faith the walls of Jericho, so too let us lift up a war cry so that in return the Lord will raise up a standard

(Isaiah 59:19 KJV) against the enemy causing him to run rampant no more.

Let us now boldly as body of believers come together touching in agreement and standing on the promise of Matthew 16:19 as we loose – in the name of Jesus Christ - the grip of every evil stronghold that calls itself wedged between the depths of hell and the promise of God's love, security, and provision. Let us then pray in its place for a binding of His holy refreshing to the faith and spirits of the body of Christ. I pray this prayer believing now that it has been answered in none other than the matchless name of our Lord and Savior, Jesus Christ. To God be all glory, and honor, and praise, Alleluia!

Quick Trips

2 Corinthians 10:3-4	1 Peter 5:8-9
Psalm 144:1	Ephesians 6:11-14
James 4:7	

Notes

_____
_____
_____

_____

Chapter Five:

Relationship

But God demonstrates His own love toward us, in that while we were yet sinners,
Christ died for us.
(Romans 5:8, NASB)

A Most Valued Possession

During my devotional two nights ago, I happened upon a verse of scripture that reconfirmed my relationship with the Lord. I was reminded of a scene in the movie X-Men when a young man, who would later grow up to be Magneto, was being separated from his parents. In desperation, his mother could not keep a firm grip on him as a group of soldiers frantically pried them apart. Though the battle was fierce, the strength of the soldiers was much too strong a force for them to bear. Needless to say, Magneto was plucked from his mother's hands. Both would never see the other again.

In pretty much the same fashion, we too have held firm grips on one thing or another in our lives. Be it the first ceramic piece we ever made in elementary school, a notebook from our favorite class in high school, or pictures of past friends with whom we are no longer in contact; the sentimental value of those items alone have had us to dub them our most prized possessions. Occasionally, due to unfortunate circumstances such as damage, theft, and/or misplacement some of those items have been lost to us forever. However, most of them do not always meet this fate.

This is because, and each in their own way, these items afford us the opportunity to relive fond memories of our glory days, share family history with the younger generations, or simply bask in the memory of what was. As a result, these valued possessions are never kept too far away from us at any given time. In an effort to protect them, some are inventoried and password enhanced. Some are listed as off limits to children or others who may not readily know their value. Some are even shielded from those we feel would either knowingly or unknowingly seek to do them harm. In other words, because of their value we seek to protect, love, and secure these items.

Let us then pretend for a moment that we are one of the above mentioned inanimate objects that is being so very well cared for. Let us pretend for a moment that we have been inventoried, secured, password protected, and deemed the most prized possession of someone with the added bonus of never being lost to theft and/or misplacement. Would that not be the most beautiful feeling of security and worth we could have? Yes, it would. Wouldn't it then stand to reason that if we would go to that extent to protect many an inanimate item of value in our lives, how much more do you think our heavenly Father would do the same for that which He created, "in His own image and likeness?" (Genesis 1:26) John 10:28-30 describes this very phenomenon in detail.

> "And I give eternal life to them, and they will never perish; and no one will snatch them out of My hand. My Father, who has given them to Me, is greater than all; and no one is able to snatch them out of the Father's hand. I and the Father are one." (NASB)

Based upon the text, we Christians should feel safe and secure in the knowledge that we are counted as Jesus' most valuable possessions. Redeemed and now off limits to the enemy, secure in our Savior's love, inventoried in the Body of Christ, and password protected from those who would knowingly or unknowingly seek to do us harm, it is evidently obvious that we are very valuable to our God, indeed. Hallelujah!

It is my prayer for each of you today that according to His promise you will never be plucked from His hand. I pray that as being counted as one of His most valuable possessions you will be able to walk in the fullness of His joy. I pray for His continued grace and mercy upon your life as He protects you from those who knowingly or unknowingly would seek to do you harm. Lastly, I pray that at all times you will know who you are in Him as well as in Whose flock you are counted. I pray this prayer believing now that it has been answered in none other than the matchless name of our Lord and Savior, Jesus Christ. To God be all glory, and honor, and praise, Alleluia!

Quick Trips

Psalm 36:5   Psalm 103:13

Romans 8:38-39   1 John 3:1

Notes

Heal me, O LORD, and I will be healed; save me and I will be saved, for You are my praise.

(Jeremiah 17:14, NASB)

And Then He Saved Me!

And then He saved me…
And my whole life was seen, pictured across my very mind;
My every gain and my every loss.
Just like someone had filmed my life and then played it back to me.
And then He saved me…
This brought back bitter memories of all the stolen romances, of all the bitter love,
Of all the words that was said in secrecy,
Of all the things whose memories hurt.
And then He saved me…
His embrace giving me a warm feeling inside as His arms pressed in gently to cover me.
Giving hope and new insights to a life whose sins and darkness
Had stolen all inner thoughts.
Now replaced with a feeling of love, belonging, and freedom never experienced before.
And then He saved me…

And I fell in love.

Glory! Alleluia

    It is my prayer for each of you today that you will rejoice in the gift of your salvation. I pray that you will look forward in excitement to the fulfillment of His promises as you acknowledge in gratitude from whence you have been delivered – never to return. Lastly, I pray His peace that surpasses all understanding upon you all. I pray this prayer believing now that it has been answered in none other than the matchless name of our Lord and Savior, Jesus Christ. To God be all glory, and honor, and praise, Alleluia!

Notes

My soul languishes for Your salvation; I wait for Your word.
My eyes fail with longing for Your word,
While I say, "When will You comfort me?"
(Psalm 119:81-82)

As the Deer...

Spring Break 2009 was one of relaxation and reconnection for my children and me. We baked, played board games, stayed up late, had movie nights, romped, and talked into the wee hours of the morning. We shared ideas and plans for the future, talked about the glory of God, and reminisced on some happy as well as not so happy times in our lives. An escape from the usual monotony of school and work, the time together was a breath of fresh air.

One caveat however, was that in getting reconnected with my children I lost contact with God. In the span of just one week, I did not interact with Him the way I did when I was on a fixed schedule. My morning worship and anointing was pushed back to the late hours of the day if at all, and my daily devotional and prayer time was almost nonexistent. As such, although I experienced His presence, I did not hear his voice. In a week, I had gone from spending a considerable amount of time with Him daily to uttering a word thanksgiving whenever the mood hit.

Caught up in the blissful moments of reconnecting with my children, I had forsaken my intimate relationship with God. As a result, I struggled with confusion and imaginations, thoughts of what-ifs, as well as my emotions. None of which were of God. After coming into this realization, I immediately repented. In an instant, I felt the return of His peace and with it the clearing of my mind. What is more, the fog that I had experienced was replaced with a soothing wave of reassurance and with it the return of His voice, "As the dear panteth for the water so should you long after Me." (Psalm 42:1)

One might ask, "What difference does a week out of His presence make?" A lot! Whenever we are not in His presence our heart – which is deceitfully wicked (Jeremiah 17:9) – chomps at the bit to take over. Additionally, we also leave room for temptations, confusion, and anxiety to creep in. Lastly, we do not readily receive what He would have said to us had we been in His presence.

For example, let us say that you are accustomed to a navigational system as your travel companion; would it be fair to say that it would be unlikely you would be able to efficiently get from point A to point B without one? Likewise, although you may dare to take to the road without it, would not the lack of the computer generated voice hinder you in getting to your final destination?

In very much the same way, being without the presence of God – even if only for a week - leaves us without the benefit of His direction. Like David it should be our mission to thirst for the living God by spending intimate time with Him in worship. In doing so, our soul would no longer have reason to cry out in sorrow, confusion, or temptation. Rather, it would be able to cry out in prayers of thanksgiving and love to the most high God. (Psalm 42)

It is my prayer for each of you today that you thirst for the living God. In doing so, I pray that you each renew your relationship with Him thus laying down your imaginations, confusions, and anxieties. I pray that in this renewed state you will avail yourself to His leading and direction. Lastly, I pray that in continually seeking Him that His presence will overcome you and bring with it a supernatural outpouring of His peace and reassurance of His promises. I pray this prayer believing now that it has been answered in none other than the matchless name of our Lord and Savior, Jesus Christ. To God be all glory, and honor, and praise, Alleluia!

Quick Trips

Psalm 63:1	Psalm 119:20, 131
Psalm 36:7-9	Psalm 34:8

Matthew 5:6   John 7:37

John 7:37   1 Peter 2:2

Revelation 21:6   Revelation 22:17

Come, let us worship and bow down,
Let us kneel before the LORD our Maker
(Psalm 95:6)

At His Feet

Celebrated as the birthday of our Lord and Savior Jesus Christ, Christmas is known as a sentimental season. In an effort to partake in age-old traditions, good food, and general Christmas cheer family and friends traverse the world to get together for the year's much anticipated festivities. Accordingly so, many of us awoke this morning to the commotion of family members rushing to the living room in anticipation of opening their packages while some, in the spirit of holiday hospitality; awoke and headed to the kitchen to complete the day's recipes. Still, there were others who awoke to the decision of whether to spend their day at one of the many family residences to which they were invited. Despite the many individual experiences however, the day began with a heightened sense of anticipation for all.

It is not uncommon however for our focus to have shifted from the birth of our Savior to the many details of the day ahead due to the hustle and bustle of preparation. Although not intentional, some of us may have gotten caught up in purchasing the perfect gift as well as the task of color coordinating the Christmas tree. Whilst still others, engrossed with the count of our guests and of the portion sizes of the food we plan to serve; become slave to the perfect party. Anxiously, many also become lost in the details left to be completed. Bound by our countless preparations, and at wits end; we become victims of exhaustion. This, my friends; is not the Lord's desire.

Found in Luke 10:38-42, the Lord was blessed when Mary chose to forsake the preparation for simply sitting at His feet. So much so, when Martha complained He told her that, "Mary had chosen the good part which will not be taken away from her." Even though Martha thought she was honoring Jesus by busying herself with multiple preparations, she had in fact lost sight of the true meaning of His visit.

Is it not pretty much the same way for us at Christmas? We busy ourselves with the task of preparation while our Lord waits patiently for us to simply come to sit at His feet. My brothers and Sisters, I challenge you this Christmas season to not be so busied with your preparations that you forget to enjoy the best seat in the house – a seat at His feet.

It is my prayer for each of you today that you do not forsake the presence of the Lord this holiday season. I pray that during your preparations you lift up a voice of worship to our God thanking Him for His most precious gift to us – His Son. Lastly, I pray that the Lord keep your families safe during this blessed holiday season. I pray this prayer believing now that it has been answered in none other than the matchless name of our Lord and Savior, Jesus Christ. To God be all glory, and honor, and praise, Alleluia!

Quick Trips

Hosea 10:12	Hosea 5:15
Psalms 27:8	Psalms 105:4
Psalms 107:19	Proverbs 28:5
2 Chronicles 7:14	2 Chronicles 15:12
Jeremiah 33:4	Isaiah 55:6
Acts 17:26-28	Matthew 6:33

Notes

And you were dead in your trespasses and sins, In which you formerly walked according to the course of this world, according to the prince of the power of the air, of the spirit that is now working in the sons of disobedience. Among them we too all formerly lived in the lusts of our flesh, indulging the desires of the flesh and of the mind, and were by nature children of wrath, even as the rest. But God, being rich in mercy, because of His great love with which He loved us, even when we were dead in our transgressions, made us alive together with Christ (by grace you have been saved), And raised us up with Him, and seated us with Him in the heavenly places in Christ Jesus, So that in the ages to come He might show the surpassing riches of His grace in kindness toward us in Christ Jesus. For by grace you have been saved through faith; and that not of yourselves, it is the gift of God; Not as a result of works, so that no one may boast.

(Ephesians 2:1-9, NASB)

But by the Grace of God

As my alarm sang obnoxiously loud one morning in an attempt to rip me from my tranquil sleep, I awoke with Marvin Sapp's *Never would Have Made It* playing in my head. Almost as a tribute to my past life, instances in which I fell short of the glory of God - and many there were - paraded themselves across my mind's eye. As I lay quietly with my thoughts, waiting for the crack that is dawn; I recounted the many instances from which had I died at that time my address would now be listed at 1 Hell's Gate, Eternal.

As I pondered my actions, it was heart wrenching to know that I had grieved God's heart for comforts that were fleeting, lusts that had passed away; people who were not my allotted portion; and recognition that was not yet mine to claim. As the memories of my sins – i.e. casual relationships, lies and envy; adulterous escapades and gossip danced around in my head it was obvious that I was on the path that led straight to destruction - my filthy rags raised high as a banner above my head.

But, as I have lived to see; 1 Corinthians 15:10 gives us all the reassurance that,

> But by the grace of God I am what I am, and His grace toward me did not prove vain; but I labored even more than all of them, yet not I, but the grace of God with me. (NASB)

Had it not been for the grace of God, and Him declaring that the enemy could go but so far and no more in my life, I shudder to think where I would be. Because of His grace, the old things have passed away; a new creation am I; a city set high on a hill for all to be drawn unto Him, and the apple of His eye are just a few of the banners I now fly high above my head in acknowledgement, praise, and gratitude to Him, the One through whom I was delivered.

So it is possible my Brothers and Sisters with each and everyone one of us for we are all called and have to the very essence of Him in whose image and likeness we have been made. In reflecting upon this I ask you, "What would you not have been able to endure if it were not for the grace extended to you by our heavenly Father? Where would you be?

In closing, Jeremiah 1:5 tells us in part that before He formed us in our mothers' womb, He knew us all by name. Luke 12:7 in part tells us that in love; even the very hairs of our heads are numbered. More so, 2 Peter 3:9 tells us that in keeping His promises the Lord is patient in judgment towards us so that none would perish but that all would come to repentance. His love, forgiveness, mercy, and grace are all yours for the asking. Claim it!

It is my prayer for each you today that you will acknowledge the hand of God in your life. As you recount the many instances in which you fell or are currently falling from grace, I pray that you will submit those instances to His mercy and forgiveness never again to have said instances held against you. It is my prayer that God will in turn raise up a standard around you declaring to the enemy that though he has been able to infiltrate your life thus far, you are no longer under his control. I decree and declare now in the name of Jesus that you have been snatched from the hands of the enemy, delivered from his trap(s), made whole, consecrated, and set aside for holy use. I pray this prayer believing now that it has been answered in none other than the matchless name of our Lord and Savior, Jesus Christ. To God be all glory, and honor, and praise, Alleluia!

Quick Trips

James 4:6   John 1:17

Romans 3:24   1 Corinthians 1:3

Titus 2:11-13

Notes

> "So then faith cometh by hearing,
> and hearing by the word of God."
> (Romans 10:17, NASB)

Comfort Food

I spent the greater part of yesterday afternoon watching the Food Network. Of the many cooking shows that aired, there was one that caught and held my attention. It was a competition that pitted four home cooks against each other for a shot of having their dish added to the menu of one of America's most popular chain restaurants. Within a set boundary of time and under the auspices of *Comfort Food*, the contestants had to prepare a delectable creation of their own invention.

As defined by pop-culture, *comfort food* is food that speaks, through our taste buds straight to our emotions. As we ingest foods that are either warm and rich in texture or sweet and creamy in taste we perceive an overwhelming sense of euphoria and well being. An option on rainy and/or rough days, comfort foods is such that, although riddled with calories; they are the first things we reach for in an attempt to quell said emotions with warmth and ecstasy from the outside in. The only problem with comfort foods however, is that the feelings of elation and well being usually eludes us as the last spoonful has been placed into our mouths. And, as the rain keeps falling or the cloud of despair returns; we either end up reaching for yet another serving to stave off the clouds or we ultimately become frustrated with the brevity of the fix. The good news however, is that there is another type of comfort Whose fix can stand the test of time and whose benefits far outweigh food.

Found not in any recipe book, nor created with any tangible ingredients this type of comfort food is accessible to all. Bound in book format, and written in many languages as well as in various versions this tangible comfort food is such that once ingested the well being and euphoria gained never leaves. Moreover, contrary to the calorie laden comfort foods described above; this comfort food has an inherent nature to fill us with warmth from the inside out. What is more, once ingested and digested it leaves a sweet and unforgettable after taste of knowledge, insight, and understanding. Lastly, although this type of comfort food is not necessarily the first thing that is reached for in times of distress and despair, it is the type that once picked up in earnest; it is hard to put down.

This comfort food my dear friends is quite simply, the Word of God – the Bible – within the pages of which lay treasures untold. Ranging from rules to live by, blessings, and instructions on how to walk daily with the Master, this comfort food – if followed - has the spiritual nutritional value of an everlasting life. Have you had your daily dose of Comfort Food today?

It is my prayer for each of you that you will set aside time daily to delve into His Word. I pray that as you do, He will use those opportunities to speak to your spirit giving you insight into His supernatural wisdom and knowledge. As you seek this knowledge and wisdom in faith, I pray that its warmth will fill you from the inside out thus giving you the boldness and courage in Him to minister to someone else. Lastly, it is my prayer that you will allow the Holy Spirit to guide your studies as you submit to the leading of the most High God. I pray this prayer believing now that it has been answered in none other than the matchless name of our Lord and Savior, Jesus Christ. To God be all glory, and honor, and praise, Alleluia!

Quick Trips

Romans 12:12	Ephesians 4:22-24
Colossians 3:1-3	Colossians 3:16
Ezekiel 36:26-27	2 Timothy 3:16
Isaiah 26:3	

> The steps of a good man are ordered by the LORD, and He delights in his way.
>
> (Psalm 37:23, NKJV)

> Everlasting trust my Lord,
> Is what I have in You.
> I see you as my caring friend,
> I do, I really do.
> Everlasting faith, my Lord,
> In which I do abide;
> Striving to delight in you,
> In your ordered, sacred stride.

It is my prayer for each of you today that you will abide in the shadow of the Almighty as He orders your steps. I pray that your obedience will delight Him. Lastly, as you submit to Him I pray that you will trust in the Lord no matter the circumstance fully knowing that He knows exactly what you need even before you ask for it. I pray this prayer believing now that it has been answered in none other than the matchless name of our Lord and Savior, Jesus Christ. To God be all glory, and honor, and praise, Alleluia!

But the one who joins himself to the Lord is one spirit with Him.
(1 Corinthians 6:17, NASB)

In Whose Flock Have You Been Counted?

The life of shepherded sheep is typically an easy one. On any given day sheep graze, rest, graze, and then rest some more; moving only when they are prompted to do so by their shepherd. The only obvious dread in a sheep's life would be falling victim to animals of prey that may venture into their immediate surroundings.

Known for their passive natures and because of their simple ways and blatant unawareness, sheep have often been deemed dumb animals. Mindless, follower, gullible, uninterested, or flighty are words akin to the characteristics of sheep. Is it not any wonder then why someone would take offense to being labeled as a sheep? On the other hand, if we were to replace the above mentioned adjectives with words to include wise, humble, trusting, guarded, or valued would being labeled as a sheep be still as insulting? I think not.

Members of the body of Christ are considered sheep. In the book of John Chapter 10:1-30 we find Jesus explaining his relationship with us using the analogy of the Shepherd and the sheep. Paraphrased, Jesus describes His sheep as knowing His voice and being called by His name. He also describes His sheep as being protected. Jesus continues to say that it is His responsibility as the shepherd to defend and shelter His sheep from thieves and robbers or from anyone who may seek to do them harm. He also promises them an abundant life.

How then can we apply the descriptors above to the role of sheep in Jesus' flock? For reflection, I posit that Jesus' sheep are indeed:

1. Wise to the life changing act of His salvation.
2. Humble enough to surrender it all to Him.
3. Trusting to know that God is above all, sovereign
4. Guarded so as not to lose the precious gift of salvation to the temptations of this world, and
5. Secure in the knowledge that we are valued by Him beyond measure.

Based on the above clarifications, do your preconceived notions of sheep now change? Jesus has already laid the foundation for us to be counted as one of His own, in His flock. He simply waits for us to hear His voice and answer the call. I ask you today, in whose flock do you dwell and, in whose flock are you counted?

It is my prayer for each of you today that you are able to renew your relationship with our Lord and Savior Jesus Christ, reestablishing your position in His most valued flock. I pray that in humility to Him, He makes your path straight and your burden light and that He shields you from any wolves that may seek your demise. Finally, as you graze daily on His Word, I pray that He infuses you with a deeper understanding of both His admonitions as well as the beauty of His promises. I pray this prayer believing now that it has been answered in none other than the matchless name of our Lord and Savior, Jesus Christ. To God be all glory, and honor, and praise, Alleluia!

Quick Trips

John 10:1-30   1 John 4:16
Colossians 1:19-20   Acts 10:34-35

Notes

_____

_____

_____

_____

I will instruct thee and teach thee in the way which thou shalt go: I will guide thee with mine eye. Be ye not as the horse, or as the mule, which have no understanding: whose mouth must be held in with bit and bridle, lest they come near unto thee.

(Psalm 32: 8-9, NKJV)

...Nothing without Him

I did not particularly have a good rest last night. My dreams were prolific. For the most part, they were simply reflections of recent events or interactions with my children. However, in the midst of them all there was one dream that stood out.

I was about twelve – a student. It was a morning like any other when my parents and I were preparing to go to school and work. I had just finished eating breakfast, and had collected my things to walk to the bus stop. I had left a few minutes early, because I wanted some time to myself to write in my diary prior to going to school. While I sat waiting on the bus, a brisk wind blew taking with it a few of my papers. As I hurried to collect them before they flew out of my reach, I happened to catch the attention of two men working nearby. Of course they wanted to help me retrieve my papers, but even in the dream I recognized these men as not being pure of heart. As such, and instead of responding to their attempts to speak to me; I began to walk back home. My pace was hurried knowing full well that if I did not catch at least one of my parents at home I would not have been able to attend school that day.

Luckily, when I arrived; my father was still there. I told him what happened and explained that although they had done nothing, I was afraid to wait on the bus with the two men standing there. In full protective mode and even without me asking, my father opted to take me to school that morning. As I got into his truck I felt safe knowing that nothing would have happened to me while I was with my father.

In the flesh someone would think of the dream as an inconsequential or as a practical adaptation of a memory from my childhood. However in the spirit, the dream entailed so much more. For example, I woke up this morning with the understanding that, in the dream, my father represented the security and protection afforded us by our heavenly Father in Psalm 91. Although I tried to get to school under my own strength I could not do so without the strength, protection, and will of my earthly father. Is that not the same premise Jesus put forth in John 5:19 when He stated,

"Therefore Jesus answered and was saying to them, "Truly, truly, I say to you, the Son can do nothing of Himself, unless it is something He sees the Father doing; for whatever the Father does, these things the Son also does in like manner." (NASB)

My Brothers and Sisters what are you trying to do without the wind of the Father in your sails? What are you trying to accomplish without first seeking His approval?

My prayer for you today is this: That all your thoughts, imaginations, and actions may be brought into alignment and obedience to the will of Christ. (2 Corinthians 10:5) I pray that all plots by the enemy against you may be canceled in the name of Jesus. I pray that angels may encamp all around you. Further, I pray that the Lord will build you up for His purposes once you come to the acknowledgement that indeed you are – we all are – nothing without Him. Lastly, I pray that you will be able to reach your true potential through Him and in Him, and all for His glory. I pray this prayer believing now that it has been answered in none other than the matchless name of our Lord and Savior, Jesus Christ. To God be all glory, and honor, and praise, Alleluia!

Quick Trips

| Psalm 91 | John 14:1 |
| Romans 8:28 | 1 Peter 5:7 |

Philippians 4:6   Psalm 138:7
2 Timothy 1:7   1 John 4:18
Psalm 21:1

When You said, "Seek My face," my heart said to You, "Your face, O Lord, I shall seek."
(Psalm 27: 8, NASB)

Reunited

It is said that as we get older we reach out to reconnect with people and places of our past hoping to make practical reconnections of what was. Nothing was made more apparent last year (2008) when I attended my high school class' twentieth reunion. Although I was not present for all the functions, the highlight of the few I did attend was reconnecting with old friends and acquaintances that had become lost in the shuffle of our adult lives.

Ripe for the picking, every function began and ended with a frantic and frenzied harvesting of phone numbers, email addresses, and web pages. In like mind, we were determined not to have the next twenty years pass us by as the first did – separate and apart from each other. Consequently, the focus shifted from gathering the information to a plan of utilizing it. As a result, popular networking websites were suggested as the hippest and most economical way to keep in touch. Excited with the opportunity to reconnect with our newly found associations, and armed with the electronic capability to do so; we were all prepared to go back to our various corners of the world.

Once home, we conversed via instant messages, photo postings, and web calls for hours at a time. Giddy with the restoration of our friendships, many of us took walks down memory lane and discussed whether or not the plans we made at seventeen had come to fruition. For some, the reunion was a much needed shot of nostalgia filled with appreciation for the return of our closest and dearest friends, and yet for others it was an opportunity to make amends for past actions as well as to forgive those who had hurt them. In the end, though short, the time was well spent. Getting reacquainted with past friends, many of whom we thought we would never see again was well worth the ticket.

Imagine then for a minute that Jesus was a member of our class - a student with whom we 'kicked' it daily? Would not He have been just as excited to be one of those with whom we were reunited? Fortunately for us and unlike my classmates and I who waited twenty years to be reunited with each other; a relationship with our Savior is always only ever a breath away. Despite our sins and non-relationship, He patiently "stands at the door and knocks" (Revelations 3:20, NASB) waiting to be invited into our hearts. Even without a travel agent to provide for plane tickets, car rentals, and/or hotel reservations the Lord is knocking at your door right now waiting to be invited in.

It is my prayer for each of you that you will fervently seek to rekindle your relationship with the Lord. As you seek Him in earnest, I pray that He will present Himself faithful in being right where He promised He would be – at your door. As you are reunited with Him, I pray that His presence will usher in a renewed sense of belonging and comfort. Lastly, I pray that the peace of the Lord be upon you all. I pray this prayer believing now that it has been answered in none other than the matchless name of our Lord and Savior, Jesus Christ. To God be all glory, and honor, and praise, Alleluia!

Quick Trips

John 17:3	Ephesians 1:17
Isaiah 43:10	1 John 1:3
Luke 10:22	James 4:7
James 1:12	Luke 11:1-4

In that day this song will be sung in the land of Judah:" We have a strong city; He sets up walls and ramparts for security.
(Isaiah 26:1, NASB)

Security under God's Protection

Upon relocating to Georgia, I took to the internet in hopes of finding a husband. Because it was not the will of my Father the search did not bear any fruit. Nonetheless, I was able to make a few acquaintances with whom I shared like interests and great conversation. Additionally, I was able to network with still others who, one way or another contributed to my walk with Christ. However as with all things in excess; there were a few hiccups along the way. Neither instrumental nor inspirational in my walk, one character in particular comes to mind. In hindsight; it is my belief that he was sent by the enemy to cause me harm.

I will never forget the evening when we first met. An affluent banker, he had invited me out to one of Atlanta's premiere dinner spots. Due to our already established rapport via telephone, conversation came easily. And so, prior to proceeding to the formal dining area; we sat in the restaurant's lounge and conversed over drinks. Among other things, we spoke about current events, family issues, and personal aspirations.

However, as the evening continued; I started to get a check in my spirit to which I did not initially respond but which got stronger the more I ignored it. Despite my growing discomfort, the evening progressed to dinner and it was not until then that things started to get weird. In the span of a few minutes my date shifted the conversation from trivial and polite banter to exclusivity and marriage, from socially acceptable behavior, to his prospective mate's dos and don'ts. In one fell swoop, it was as if Dr. Jeckle had left the room, and Mr. Hyde had sat down with me.

If that weren't bizarre enough, he started speaking about a list of places we could go to visit that coming week, as well as about flying out to meet his parents the very next weekend. But the icing on the cake, and the reason for the blaringly bright red flag that was frantically being waved over my head; came when he pressed me to follow him home that evening. Despite my repeated denial, he continued to push until finally he lost his temper. Although scared to jelly on the inside, however seemingly quite in control on the outside; I ended the evening much to his vocal dismay. And just as if God had erased my name and contact information out of his mind, he was never heard from again.

Glory to God! In retrospect, I now shudder to think what would have happened if I had trustingly followed him home that night. Would I even be sitting here pondering the outcome?

It is often said that God takes care of babes and fools, but quoted in Psalm 91, there is an assured protection for those who dwell within the secret place of the most high God. My Brothers and Sisters, do you dwell in that secret place? And if so, from what has God protected you? It may very well be that His grace was such that the danger did not even get a chance to rear its ugly head. However, even in circumstances in which you are aware of seemingly impending danger take courage that even though "the devil , as a roaring lion walks along seeking whom he may devour;" (1 Peter 5:8) "though a thousand fall at your side, and ten thousand at your right hand, near you it shall not come." (Psalm 91:7) Alleluia!

It is my prayer for each of you today that you will lift praises to the living God first acknowledging Him as the gatekeeper of your lives and then thanking Him for His protection. I pray that in all things you will lean not to your own understanding, or wants, or desires, but that in trusting in Him He will direct your paths. (Proverbs 3:5-6). Lastly, I pray the blessing of Isaiah 54:17 on each of your lives today and always. I pray this prayer believing now that it has been answered in none other than the matchless name of our Lord and Savior, Jesus Christ. To God be all glory, and honor, and praise, Alleluia!

Quick Trips

Numbers 6:24-26   Isaiah 35:4
Psalm 81:1-2   Psalm 18:30
Romans 8:38-39   Philippians 4:7
Psalm 91

Notes

I will hear what God the LORD will say; for He will speak peace to His people, to His godly ones; but let them not turn back to folly.

(Psalm 85:8, NASB)

Speak, Lord...

Just this past weekend, I received a love letter from God. During Saturday morning's devotional, I was led to my Bible's front cover in which my mother had placed an inscription. Dated a little over a year and a half ago on May 29, 2007, the inscription simply read, "To Danie." Under it was the scriptural reference to Jeremiah 29: 11-14 which reads,

> "For I know the plans that I have for you," declares the LORD." Plans for welfare and not for calamity to give you a future and a hope. Then you will call upon Me and come and pray to Me, and I will listen to you. You will seek Me and find Me when you search for Me with all your heart. I will be found by you, "declares the LORD, 'and I will restore your fortunes and will gather you from all the nations and from all the places where I have driven you," declares the LORD, "and I will bring you back to the place from where I sent you into exile." (NASB)

Overwhelmed with emotion, I immediately fell prostrate and started to worship. It was simply amazing that God would have me to discover, at the right time; a word He left for me via my mother a year and a half ago. Just the week before, I had struggled with God's timing of blessings in my life, but here it was just a few days later He was reminding me yet again of another one of His promises. My God!

Have you ever received a word from the Lord that seems to strike just the right chord in your spirit? Whether it be via His written word, through our hearts, audibly, or via a word from a member of the body of Christ; God indeed speaks to His people. Throughout the Bible, as well as all through history via His prophets; God has made His word, wishes, directives, and plans known to us. The key however to availing ourselves to the many avenues through which He speaks would be (1) being expectant for the word; (2) seeking confirmation through the discernment of the Holy Spirit; and (3) once tried by the Spirit, receiving it in obedience.

Evidenced in 1 Samuel 3 God spoke to Samuel via Eli's prompting to be receptive to God. Through the command, "Speak Lord, for your servant is listening" Samuel made himself open to God's word. Had Samuel first not been obedient to Eli, or even receptive to God's word neither the legacy of King David nor the birth of Joseph – husband of Mary the mother of our Lord – would have come to fruition.

Similarly, had I not been expectant for and receptive to Jeremiah 29: 11 – 14, the glory of God would not have rested on me this weekend as I basked in yet another one of His promises. What is more, the Word would not have been able to take root in my spirit where it would ultimately grow, and sustain my faith in Him until His perfect will be made manifest in my life. As such my Brothers and Sisters, the question for you today then becomes how expectant for, receptive to, and fertile are you to receiving a Word from the Lord?

It is my prayer for each of you today that you open your hearts in expectation for what God would want to say to you. In inviting Him to speak, I pray that He will speak to your spirit in ways you have never experienced before. Lastly, it is my prayer that His glory be deposited upon you so that you may rest assured in His promises for your life as you continue to walk in covenant with Him and according to His commandments. I pray this prayer believing now that it has been answered in none other than the matchless name of our Lord and Savior, Jesus Christ. To God be all glory, and honor, and praise, Alleluia!

Quick Trips

Acts 22:14　　　　　Genesis 3:8

Isaiah 30:21	John 10:3
Romans 8:14	Hebrews 3:7-8
John 16:8	Deuteronomy 4:35-36
Psalm 95:17	Daniel 11:32

Song of Solomon 2:14

_____
_____
_____
_____
_____
_____
_____
_____
_____
_____
_____
_____
_____
_____
_____

Moses built an altar and named it The LORD is My Banner; and he said, "The LORD has sworn; the LORD will have war against Amalek from generation to generation."
(Exodus 17:15-16, NASB)

The Only One That Matters

It is no secret that we are social creatures. One does not have to look far to support that premise. From cook-outs to Sunday dinner, formal affairs to casual get-togethers we are constantly in a state of flux seeking the next function, the next big outing with friends. As a result, this leads many of us to seek affiliation with and/or pledge our allegiance to organizations in an effort to simply belong.

In an attempt to publicize our newly procured memberships, we often color coordinate our wardrobes; wear pins on our lapels, as well as place decals, license plates and/or frames on our cars so that they can be seen as we travel proudly from point A to point B. If that were not enough, some of us even tattoo ourselves with the organization's emblem signifying our undying devotion, as prescribed by the pledge that we took, even up until our death.

Considered normal by today's standard, and even expected by most, these are the just some of the ways many of us raise banners of association above our head, pledges made to the world in exchange for group perks. What is sad about this is that the same acknowledgement that is given to the perks derived from the banners of the world is not given in reverence to the banner of God. As advised in Psalm 60:4, the banner of the Lord should be raised for the purpose of staving off wars as well as for embracing His love (Song of Solomon 2:4.)

Is it any wonder then that even within the institutions that we love and cherish so dearly there is strife among us, rivalry amongst the brethren, as members jockey for position? The direct result of which is waged wars and broken promises? Contrary to the banners of the world, God's banner of love and protection can never be broken.

My brothers and sisters what banner is it that you have proudly emblazoned upon your chest, or lifted high above your head? Is it the banner of the living God? Or have you defined yourself according to the banners of the gods of this world.

It is my prayer for each of you today that you are able to lift high the banner of the living God in testament of who and Whose you are. I pray then that all wars waged against you will be no more, and that the love of God will be poured out upon and manifested through you so that others may be called unto Him.

Lastly, I pray His banner be lifted high over you at all times as a signal of both your trust in and the glory of God as He blesses and protects you and your family for generations and generations to come. I pray this prayer believing now that it has been answered in none other than the matchless name of our Lord and Savior, Jesus Christ. To God be all glory, and honor, and praise, Alleluia!

Quick Trips

Exodus 17:15	Psalm 20:5
Psalm 60:4	Isaiah 11:10
Jeremiah 50:2	Jeremiah 51:27

Jeremiah 4:6

Notes

Wait on the LORD: be of good courage,
and he shall strengthen thine heart: wait, I say, on the LORD.
(Psalm 27:14, NKJV)

Wait!

Subscription to *BlackPeopleMeet.com*, $5.95 a month
Subscription to *Yahoomeet.com*, $12.95 a month
Subscription to *eharmony.com*, $19.99 a month
Waiting on the Lord to present you with your mate…
Priceless!

It is my prayer for those of you today desiring a mate that you will let patience have her perfect way with you that you will be made whole – wanting nothing. (James 1:4). I pray that you will use this time to draw closer to the Lord as you wait for the mate He has ordained for you. As you develop your relationship with Him during this time of preparation, I pray that He will reveal the areas in your life in need of realignment to His word. Lastly, I pray that you will submit yourself to the leading of the Holy Spirit as you humbly embrace the revelations brought forth as a lesson in love from our heavenly Father. I pray this prayer believing now that it has been answered in none other than the matchless name of our Lord and Savior, Jesus Christ. To God be all glory, and honor, and praise, Alleluia!

Quick Trips

Psalm 37:9	Psalm 37:16
Psalm 39:7	Psalm 52:8-9
Psalm 62:1-12	Psalm 145:15
Proverbs 20:22	Lamentations 3:25

Notes

How much better it is to get wisdom than gold! And to get understanding is to be chosen above silver.

(Proverbs 16:16, NASB)

Wisdom and Understanding

Growing up I was a bit 'fast' in the mouth. Although not a mischievous or overly disgusting child my words were always quick and my responses like a whip. Because of this, I often found myself at the receiving end of my mother's back hand. Convinced that her favorite scripture was Proverbs 13:24; I ducked and weaved in an effort to avoid her blows – of course to no avail.

What is more, as opposed to simply changing my ways, I sometimes dared to ask why she was so adamant on enforcing her law. Her response, and what I would guess was her second favorite scripture, was always;

> "For whom the LORD loveth He correcteth; even as a father the son in whom he delighteth. Happy is the man that findeth wisdom, and the man that getteth understanding. For the merchandise of It Is better than the merchandise of silver and the gain thereof than fine gold." (Proverbs 3:12-14, NKJ)

Consequently, for daring to question her authority, she would paraphrase word by word, "If I didn't love you, I wouldn't correct you!", as she landed lash after lash. This, I suppose, was her way of reminding me just how much she abided in this scripture.

Although those years are now gone, I often look back in hindsight grateful that my mother cared enough to discipline me. Through many tears, I was able to learn the value of respect, trustworthiness, and honor – just to name a few. Further, because she delighted in me, I was able to grow up to be a respectable, contributing member of society – a child in whom she is well pleased.

In pretty much the same way our heavenly Father who wishes to delight in us, admonishes us from time to time. Similar to the way a mother doe nudges her newborn baby in getting it to try out its new legs, our Father leads us along life's many turns away from the things that ultimately lead to damnation and towards the things that will bring us closer to Him. Found in Matthew 7:11 His position is, "If ye then, being evil, know how to give good gifts unto your children, how much more shall your Father which is in heaven give good things to them that ask Him?"

This does not mean however that the Lord will give us a signed blank check. Similar to my mother's desire for me, the Lord would have us to forsake our wicked ways, avail ourselves to His salvation, walk in covenant and develop an intimate relationship with Him. When we do, we will be able to gain heavenly insight into His wisdom and understanding as evidenced in Proverbs 2:6.

> "The Lord gives wisdom; from His mouth come knowledge and understanding." (NASB)

In closing, it should be the desire of all Christians to seek both wisdom and understanding as,

> "By wisdom a house is built, and by understanding it is established; and by knowledge the rooms are filled with all precious and pleasant riches." (Proverbs 24:3-4, NASB)

It is my prayer for each of you today that you continuously seek His counsel in an effort to gain wisdom and understanding in the things of God. I pray that as He mercifully chastens you, you will heed to His leading as He points you in the direction you should go. Lastly, it is my prayer that as you submit to God's holy wisdom that all the rooms of your steadily established house be filled, "with all precious and pleasant riches." I pray this prayer believing now that it has been answered in none other than the matchless name of our Lord and Savior, Jesus Christ. To God be all glory, and honor, and praise, Alleluia!

Quick Trips

Psalm 119:34	Psalm 90:12
Proverbs 28:26	Proverbs 23:4
Proverbs 4:7	1 Corinthians 1:19, 24

1 Corinthians 3:19   Luke 24:45
James 1:15   James 3:17

Notes

Chapter Six:
The Promises of God

And my God will supply all your needs according to His riches in glory in Christ Jesus.
(Philippians 4:19, NASB)

Believing in God's Provision

During these uncertain economic times, some of us have been relegated to live from paycheck to paycheck in an effort to make ends meet. Some have even found themselves - through no choice of their own - making bids for the few jobs that are available in today's market. As a consequence, many are left to sit idly by as the bills stack up on the coffee table whilst others are left to become professional jugglers opting instead to alternate the payment of their bills. If that weren't enough, and in adding insult to injury; some are also forced to dodge calls from disgruntled creditors or bill collectors who - in the right - are seeking to secure what is theirs. And so it happens, almost in an endless loop of stacking, alternating, and dodging; that the saga of living in frustration and anxiety goes - for some without any end in sight.

The good news in accordance with Matthew 6: 25 - 34 is that we are all encouraged not to be anxious because of God's provision for His children. The apostle Matthew wrote,

"For this reason I say to you, do not be worried about your life, as to what you will eat or what you will drink; nor for your body, as to what you will put on. Is not life more than food and the body more than clothing? Look at the birds of the air, that they do not sow, nor reap nor gather into barns, and yet your heavenly Father feeds them. Are you not worth much more than they?
And who of you by being worried can add a single hour to his life? And why are you worried about clothing? Observe how the lilies of the field grow; they do not toil nor do they spin, yet I say to you that not even Solomon in all his glory clothed himself like one of these. "But if God so clothes the grass of the field, which is alive today and tomorrow is thrown into the furnace, will He not much more clothe you? You of little faith! "Do not worry then, saying, 'What will we eat?' or 'What will we drink?' or 'What will we wear for clothing?'" "For the Gentiles eagerly seek all these things; for your heavenly Father knows that you need all these things. "But seek first His kingdom and His righteousness, and all these things will be added to you. "So do not worry about tomorrow; for tomorrow will care for itself. Each day has enough trouble of its own."

Consequently, and as cliché as it may sound; the statement "One day at a time," is founded in biblical principal. We are encouraged in knowing that our heavenly Father - our Jehovah-Jireh, who provides for the seemingly miniscule things of this earth; will also be sure to provide for us, His children, if we but seek Him first and all His righteousness. In other words, our Spiritual Daddy already knows what we need to make it and in exactly what portion, "one day at a time."

Why then should we worry about tomorrow? It is His will that we do not. In walking in faith with Him it should be our position as the body of Christ that all of our daily needs are met. As we pray, "Give us this day our daily bread" we should take courage that in God's omniscience all things have already been, "Worked out for the good of those who love Him and to those who are called to His purpose." (Romans 8:28)

It is my prayer for each of you today that you will trust Him always. I pray that you will be made confident in the knowledge that our heavenly Father is indeed sovereign and has already doled out the necessary portion needed for your daily success. I pray that in true reflection you will come to the realization of how many times your needs have been met and that you lift up your hands in a praise of thanksgiving to the Most High God. Lastly, I pray – standing on the promise of Matthew 16:19 - that your anxiety be bound in the name of Jesus Christ our Savior, and that the peace that surpasses all understanding be released in its place (Philippians 4:7). I pray this prayer believing that it has been answered in none other than the matchless name of our Lord and Savior, Jesus Christ our Savior. To God be all glory, honor, and praise, Alleluia!

Quick Trips

Psalm 111:5   Deuteronomy 28:12

Psalm 132:15   2 Corinthians 9:10

1 Timothy 5:8   Luke 12:24

Notes

I sought Your favor with all my heart;
Be gracious to me according to Your word.
(Psalm 119:58)

Exceeding, Abundantly

One year ago (2008), the Lord blessed my children and me with a beautiful home. It all began on a Saturday morning running errands from one side of the town to the next. As I passed by what is currently my subdivision, an audible voice invaded my senses.

"Turn in," the voice said.

And just as quick as the voice had spoken I responded in haste,

"No, I will not. I don't want to live here."

Just a few weeks later when passing by the same subdivision, I once again heard the voice as it spoke as clear as day.

"Turn in."

This time and in reverence, I acknowledged the voice as Whose it was and obediently turned in. Driving in to the subdivision, I could not get over just how peaceful and serene the environment was. En route to the sales office, I offered up a word of prayer. In my mind, I was not prepared to step into a venture of this proportion, nonetheless; by His leading here I was.

As I walked into the sales room, my head astir with questions, I was met by the most energetic, yet welcoming sales representative I have ever met. Brief introductions were made as she gave me a tour of the two furnished models. Curious to see if I was interested in purchasing a home, she invited me to see the unfurnished models that were ready for habitation. I accepted, and off we went. Touring home after home and model after model we finally came to rest on the street I currently live.

Because of their location, there were only two houses on the street that appealed to me. As I entered the first one, it was dark and cold, and the view was not what I expected. Seeing the dissatisfaction on my face, the sales agent quickly prompted for us to move to the model across the street, and as I pushed the front door and entered; I was met with an overwhelming sense of warmth.

The warmth was then replaced with a peace I have never experienced before and with it came His voice once again,

"You are home."

Overwhelmed with emotion, tears began to stream down my face. As the children excitedly ran around the house claiming their bedrooms, I simply stood in awe of God and silently worshiped Him.

Fifteen minutes later, I made a minimal down payment on the house and, even though I struggled in faith worrying about how the home was going to be financed, the Lord made it so that the loan was approved without any difficulties. The closing took place twenty one days later, and despite the initial estimate of a substantial amount of money needed for closing; I went to the table with nothing in hand. Talk about favor! Hallelujah!

In closing, just as He has promised God is able to do, "Exceeding, abundantly above all that we ask or think, according to the power that worketh in us," (Ephesians 3:20, KJV) for those who walk in covenant with and abide by His commandments.

It is my prayer today that God will pour out His blessings upon you according to His riches in heaven. I pray that they will be exceeding, abundantly more than anything you could ever have imagined. I pray that no matter the shape, size, or form the blessing may take that you will receive it graciously, lifting up a hand of gratitude and praise to the most high God. Lastly, I pray that you will always walk in a spirit of expectance so that you will never miss an opportunity to be blessed by Him. Finally and in agreement, let us now lift up a concerted praise of gratitude to Him for everything He has ever done for us. I pray this prayer believing now that it has been answered in none other than the matchless name of our Lord and Savior, Jesus Christ. To God be all glory, and honor, and praise, Alleluia!

Quick Trips

Deuteronomy 28	Psalm 5:12
Galatians 3:14	Proverbs 10:6

Proverbs 28:20   Psalm 41:1

Notes

I set My bow in the cloud, and it shall be for a sign of a covenant between Me and the earth.

(Genesis 9:13, NASB)

We all have heard the phrase,
"When it rains, it pours."
Mostly in times of abundance and joy.
But we never seem to realize
For we take it for granted,
That sorrow, misery, and abandonment can suddenly hit
With the same impact and intensity
As a thunderous storm.
Just as well, we seem to forget the faith and hope
That was given to us by the Almighty Creator,
In whose image and likeness we were made.
We forget our endurance, we forget our stamina,
And most importantly; we forget the gift that He gave to us
On the night of His betrayal
In times of darkness, especially when we need it the most.
He has given us the tool of prayer
To use as a people, not only when it is feasible to us;
But also to praise and give Him thanks for the simple things we

Take for granted like RAINBOWS.
We do know how the power of just one prayer
Can change all things and alter all destinies.
But, prayer should not only be the first thing we turn to
In times of need.
It should be first and foremost on our minds and lips.
Let there always be a song of praise and thanksgiving
On your tongues offered to the Lord for the things that He has given.
And keep in mind; that in times of darkness before turning to worldly solutions,
Reach to the heavens.
Just as well as in times of abundance,
Truly render your hearts and your petitions to the Almighty
Standing firm on His promises of better to come.
For through Him,
All things are possible;
And,
After a storm, a rainbow shines through!

It is my prayer for each of you today that you are able to commune with the Lord on a daily basis. I pray that in speaking with Him, you will never forget the wildernesses in your lives out of which He has brought you. I pray that as you lift up your words of praise and thanksgiving that He will accept them as a sweet, sweet fragrance and count them toward your continued favor. Lastly, it is my prayer that no matter the circumstance, praise will be first and foremost on your lips. I pray this prayer believing now that it has been answered in none other than the matchless name of our Lord and Savior, Jesus Christ. To God be all glory, and honor, and praise, Alleluia!

Quick Notes

Psalm 141:2	Psalm 86:6
Psalm 4:1	Psalm 6:9
Matthew 18:19-20	Matthew 5:44
James 5:16	Luke 21:36
Ephesians 6:18	Romans 8:26

Notes

If we say that we have fellowship with Him and yet walk in the darkness, we lie and do not practice the truth; but if we walk in the Light as He Himself is in the Light, we have fellowship with one another, and the blood of Jesus His Son cleanses us from all sin.
(1 John 1:5-7, NASB)

God's Promise of Fellowship

This weekend, through prayer and fellowship with my daughter, son, and a few close friends, I was able to encounter God on a whole new level. As mentioned in the previous article entitled, *It's All in His Name*, God shows Himself mighty and present whenever His name is called upon. He does this even more so when it is done in fellowship with other believers in the body of Christ and in agreement. Evidenced in Matthew 18: 19 - 20, our Father tells us,

> "Again I say unto you, that if two of you shall agree on earth as touching anything that they shall ask, it shall be done for them of my Father which is in heaven. For where two or three are gathered together in my name, there am I in the midst of them."

Consequently, this tells us that as believers of Christ we should not forsake the congregational fellowship for it is within those parameters that God also shows himself present and mighty all the more.

Accordingly so, it should behoove any of you who may have let go of the congregational fellowship to resume post haste. It is in this fellowship that we are washed clean and extorted by the Body of Christ. It is in fellowship that we are healed. It is in fellowship that we are delivered. It is in fellowship that we can be safe in spiritual warfare. It is in fellowship that the spirit of the Lord dwells. As such, whether you are in the process of seeking God's will for your life, deliverance, guidance, or comfort do so in the midst of fellowship.

It is my prayer for each of you today that you do not forsake the promise of fellowship granted to us by God. I pray that all your needs and desires will be met according to His will and portion for your life in the fellowship with members of the body of Christ. It is my prayer that in seeking Him first, everything else will be added unto you (Matthew 6:33). It is also my prayer for you today, that the Holy Spirit will guide you to like persons in Him so that your true congregational fellowship and worship may begin. Finally, it is my prayer that through fellowship you will be made whole and drawn closer to Him. I pray this prayer believing that it has been answered in none other than the matchless name of our Lord and Savior, Jesus Christ our Savior. To God be all glory, honor, and praise, Alleluia!

Quick Trips

Acts 2:42, 44-47   Hebrews 10: 24-25

Philippians 2:14   2 Corinthians 6:14

1 John 1:6

Notes

> But if anyone loves God, he is known by Him
> (1 Corinthians 8:3)

Priceless

    Many of us have seen the Master Card commercials in which the results of various scenarios are deemed priceless in their presented context. Of the many, my favorite commercial is entitled "Dinner Out." In this scenario the kitchen and all its accoutrements whoop it up while their owners go out to enjoy a quiet dinner. The knives take in a scary movie; the pot spoons spend time in a make shift hot tub, and the ingredients dance together on the marble kitchen counters as the couple charge the cost of dinner on their Master Card. As the couple return home however, the bits and pieces hurriedly pack themselves up so as not to be found out. In the end and even though money was spent, both the couple and the kitchen utensils enjoyed a much needed evening off – priceless!

    Similarly, we all have had many life experiences upon which we can place either a monetary or sentimental value. Although precious in our eyes, those experiences however should pale in comparison to the day we find and ultimately surrender our lives to the Lord and Savior Jesus Christ. Similar to the metamorphosis of a caterpillar who endures three stages prior to emerging the new creation it was purposed to be, our transformation upon submitting to our Father should be a living testament of the newness and rededication of our lives. From the initial stage of first proclaiming Christ through to the process of being made whole and blameless to stand before Him; our walk with God should be so breathtakingly beautiful - a sight for all to see - that it is an outward fulfillment of the promise of 2 Corinthians 5:17.

> "Therefore if anyone is in Christ, he is a new creature; the old things passed away; behold, new things have come." (NASB)

Thus, our desire as Christians should be to become a new creation in Him – our daily prayer to decrease so that He may increase (John 3:30, NASB). By doing so, we will allow the old things to pass away leaving room for Him to pour into us what He has designed us to be - the purpose for our existence on earth. What my Brothers and Sisters, could be more priceless than that - to walk in the promise of His perfect will for our lives?

It is my prayer for each of you today that you are able to die to yourself leaving room for the Lord to fill you with the leading and the purpose of the Holy Spirit. I pray that within each and every one of your cocoons there is a brand new creation bursting at the seams to be released into his/her purpose. I also pray that you will never look back upon the old ways, paths, or things of your lives as they have been passed away and made void by the Lord. Lastly, I pray that you will lay a claim to your birth right, the purpose and plan God has for your life never allowing the enemy to get a hold of it. I pray this prayer believing now that it has been answered in none other than the matchless name of our Lord and Savior, Jesus Christ. To God be all glory, and honor, and praise, Alleluia!

Quick Trips

Romans 13:11-12	Romans 6:4
2 Corinthians 5:17	Galatians 2:20
Jeremiah 29:11-14	Psalm 103:12
Romans 14:7	

Notes

_____
_____
_____
_____
_____
_____

Chapter Seven:

Encouragement

The end of a matter is better than its beginning;
patience of spirit is better than haughtiness of spirit.
(Ecclesiastes 7:8, NASB)

Let Patience Have Her Perfect Way...

One of the most fulfilling times in my life has been the fourteen years I have spent in the classroom as an elementary school teacher. What is more, I have enjoyed being a part of the growth of the many students whom I have had the privilege to call my own. The happy sounds of their laughter as well as the luminescence of their faces whenever understanding is gained will forever be engrained upon my memory.

But, unless you are a teacher; one cannot imagine the documentation and piles of paperwork that is involved. And despite the hearts and flowers, the act of teaching and the many administrative tasks it entails do have a way of becoming very daunting, sometimes downright tedious. Imagine a job so consuming that it would require two eight hour shifts to accomplish what is required in only one. Accordingly so, and after teaching for several years; the monotony slowly builds until finally one literally wants to run down the hallways screaming, "Let me up on outta here!"

A victim of *nextitis*, an irresistible compulsion to move on to something else; I am constantly chomping at the bit for the next big, new thing to do. Having no shortage of ideas due to the many things God has placed upon my heart, I often look forward in excitement to the fruition of His promises. In an attempt to achieve them however, I often find myself scaling back responsibilities in other areas of my life to make room – so to speak – for the new things. As a result, I often struggle to balance my already heavy plate with one hand while reaching for the promises of God with the other.

Not the will of God, what I failed to realize was that God would not have me to forsake the enjoyment of my now to chase after a vision that has not yet been scheduled for manifestation. Rather, He would have me to minister whole heartedly to those in whose direct line of interaction I had been placed – i.e. my students, my parents, my colleagues, and my administrators. As it stands, in being, "sober in all things, enduring hardship, and doing the work of an evangelist," I am ultimately fulfilling my God appointed ministry in His perfect time. (2 Timothy 4:5, NASB)

My Brothers and Sisters, what drudgery do you endure at work that hinders you from ministering whole heartedly to your colleagues? What visions are you chasing whose time it is not yet to be manifested?

It is my prayer for each of you today that you use your God appointed position to minister to those in need. I pray that as you wholeheartedly fulfill your ministry, you will be rewarded according to your works. Lastly and in regards to His promises to you, I pray that you will let patience have her perfect work in you, so that you may be perfect and entire, wanting nothing. (James 1:4) I pray this prayer believing now that it has been answered in none other than the matchless name of our Lord and Savior, Jesus Christ. To God be all glory, and honor, and praise, Alleluia!

Quick Trips

Luke 18:15	Luke 21:19
Romans 5:3	Romans 8:25
Hebrews 2:3	Hebrews 10:23
James 1:3	Colossians 3:12
Habakkuk 2:3	

Notes

_____
_____
_____

Therefore be imitators of God, as beloved children; and walk in love, just as Christ also loved you and gave Himself up for us, an offering and a sacrifice to God as a fragrant aroma.

But immorality or any impurity or greed must not even be named among you, as is proper among saints; and there must be no filthiness and silly talk, or coarse jesting, which are not fitting, but rather giving of thanks.

(Ephesians 5:1-4, NASB)

Merriment or Reverence:

You Decide

Like Christmas, Easter is another Christian holiday whose meaning has become totally desensitized through commercialism. As opposed to truly reflecting upon the ultimate sacrifice made for us, many rush to the stores in droves to purchase eggs, grass, bunny rabbits, and baskets. Not too far behind in purchases are liquor, paper goods, and food items as many get set for a weekend of partying and drunken merriment in the spirit of revelry. Ultimately, the meaning of the most solemn of acts ever endured by our Master is remembered not by reverence in sincere and grateful hearts but by greed, drunkenness, and glee. This is sad for were it not for the love Christ has for us all there would not have been an Easter to celebrate, no reason to socialize. As such, and directly correlated to this premise; I ask a simple question that many have struggled with throughout the years, "What came first? Was it the chicken or was it the egg?"

In this case, and as believers, we know that it was His love, His sacrifice that came first. Because of His sacrifice we are now the benefactors of that most precious gift – the gift of salvation. Because of His sacrifice, we are able to claim dominion over the things of this world – including, but not limited to; lack, loss, illness, disease, and death. Because of Him, we are now joint heirs to the throne. (John 15:13 -15, Romans 8:14-17)

Would it then not behoove us to acknowledge first the meaning of the season, prior to engaging in worldly pleasures? Would it then not prosper our spirits to give thanks to the very One by Whose actions it is we are able to live life and live it this abundantly? It is written,

> "Seek ye first His kingdom and His righteousness, and all these things will be added unto you." (Matthew 6:33, NASB)

My Brothers and Sisters, why then are we not seeking Him first during this most sacred of times? Why have our spirits been led astray, colluding with the world in order to minimize, or worse; forget the ultimate sacrifice that was made for us?

It is my prayer for each of you today that you will be renewed in the mind as to the true meaning of the Resurrection season. I pray that as you solemnly, yet gratefully reflect upon the Resurrection's true meaning that there will always be a word of praise and thanksgiving in your mouth. Further, I pray that your gratefulness will be sustained at all times and not just relegated to the length of this weekend. Lastly, as you go about your days I pray the boldness of the Lord upon you as you spread the good news to those who may have forgotten, or those who simply may not know. I pray this prayer believing now that it has been answered in none other than the matchless name of our Lord and Savior, Jesus Christ. To God be all glory, and honor, and praise, Alleluia!

Quick Trips

Exodus 32:1-10   Deuteronomy 21:20
Proverbs 23:29-30   Isaiah 22:13-14

Notes

Thou therefore, my son, be strong in the grace that is in Christ Jesus

(2 Timothy 2:1)

More Than a Conqueror!

For as long as I can remember, I have started every New Year with an extensive list of resolutions. Vowing to change one thing or another, each year has always begun with a renewed sense of purpose. Determined to adopt such changes, I journal my plans in an effort to incorporate a more organized, healthy lifestyle. And so, with much attention to detail; the first few months are executed flawlessly - a piece of cake.

As the novelty of the New Year wanes however, and my daily routine starts to take on a life of its own; the resolutions fade and so does my determination to execute them. Usually by April, a sense of frustration and failure sets in and, try as I might; I cannot reinstate my resolutions with the same zeal with which they were initially planned. All forlorn, I give up to purportedly end the vicious cycle – until next year, that is.

Accordingly so, set in place as solutions to bad habits; resolutions are sometimes more problematic than once anticipated. The old cliché, "Old habits die hard" is one such indicator. In as much as our intentions to change may be sincere, the actual process through which we do is difficult. One caveat of this is failure.

For example, how many of you have started a new year hoping to quit smoking, lose weight, or begin the year with a functioning budget only to find that by midyear you have fallen into the same old habits you were trying to break? In the end and victim to a loss of self confidence brought on by your lack of will power your New Year's resolutions are placed on the back burner as you focus your attention on other things.

The good news in the midst of this vicious cycle however, is that words of encouragement can be found in the Bible. Here are a few examples:

> I can do all things through Christ who strengthens me. (Philippians 4:13)
>
> Yet in all these things, we are more than conquerors through Him who loved us. (Romans 8:37)
>
> Ye are of God, little children, and have overcome them: because greater is He that is in you, than he that is in the world. (1 John 4:4)
>
> Being confident of this very thing, that He which hath begun a good work in you will perform it until the day of Jesus Christ (Philippians 1:6)

In an effort to facilitate us in conquering anything that would separate us from Him or otherwise cause us stress, the Lord has etched within the pages of the Good Book a recipe for us to stand steadfast and purposed to the things we wish to change.

Personally, my favorite of the above listed scriptures is Philippians 1:6. In this scripture, we are reassured that the good work the Lord has started within us will be completed. Stated best in Mary, Mary's *I Just Can't Give up Now*, though the road may be long and the battles many God will never leave me or forsake me (Hebrews 13:5). As Christians, we should prescribe to the promise that our God would "not have brought us this far to leave us." Thus, found in 1Timothy 4:7 our slogan for conquering New Year's resolutions – among other things - should be to fight the good fight, finish the course, and keep the faith. In conclusion my Brothers and Sisters, what goals have you set for yourself this New Year? And most importantly, by whose steam will you conquer those goals?

It is my prayer for each of you today that the Lord will reveal anything that He would have you change this New Year. In submitting to His will, I pray that you will be encouraged through the valleys and the mountains that you will endure. I also pray that you will allow Him to be the wind under your wings as you journey onto victory. Lastly, I pray that you will always remember that you are more than a conqueror through Christ, a child of the living God. I pray this prayer believing now that it has been answered in none other than the matchless name of our Lord and Savior, Jesus Christ. To God be all glory, and honor, and praise, Alleluia!

Quick Trips

Romans 8:37	Proverbs 16:3
Psalm 37:5	Psalms 84:12
Isaiah 26:4	Isaiah 26:3

Notes

> Death and life are in the power of the tongue,
> and those who love it will eat its fruit.
> (Proverbs 18:21, NASB)

Spoken Words

As a panacea for those who would resort to violence in the defense of their names, Judge Judy often recites the old adage, "Sticks and stones may break my bones, but words will never harm me." In like fashion, parents also speak the same in comfort to upset children who complain of harsh words spoken to them by their peers. Conversely and as our individual experiences would dictate, nothing could be further from the truth. Negative words can and do hurt.

Words are such that they can either soothe, or destroy; calm, or stir; build up, or break down; encourage, or send astray. Coincidently, they can be the things nightmares are made of, or conversely; a fertile land for such things as excellence, achievement, or legacy. Words are the lattices upon which bridges of lasting memories – good or bad - can be formed, or a shovel with which graves of a once bright future gone awry can be dug. In short, words are the vehicles through which our emotions, encouragement, love, friendship, fears, insecurities, jealousies, punishments, and/or wickedness are visited upon others, and although many may beg to differ; words are indeed alive.

In examining some general scenarios in our own lives how many times have you been the recipient of words that have pierced you to the bone only to shrug it off as if it never happened but later found yourself debating whether or not there was any truth to the offensive phrases? How many times have you either cried, become bitter, or reacted overly defensive to things that had been said? More so, how many times have you recalled painful words that had been spoken years before only to still remember how much they hurt?

Many, if not all of us; have experienced at least one of the above mentioned scenarios in which there was some sort of reaction to negativity. Why then would one choose to think that negative words do not hurt when as we have noted they always tend to bring about an act of defense? You see, the thing with word wounds is that they are not physically apparent. For example, if you were in the presence of a person who had lost a limb due to an unforeseen accident, their wound, or rather; the result of their wound would be clearly visible. Unfortunately, such is not the same for those who have been marred by words. This is why it is vitally important for us as Christians that we use our words not to cause any further damage to those whose wounds we cannot see, but rather to build up in all things as well as to encourage.

As Christians we must begin to pour into those around us as dictated in the following two verses in the book of Proverbs. These two verses give us some well needed, practical advice for delivering our words.

> "A soft answer turneth away wrath: but grievous words stir up anger." Proverbs 15:1 (KJV)

> "Pleasant words are as a honeycomb, sweet to the soul, and health to the bones." Proverbs 16:24 (NASB)

In short, when dealing with others, Christians should be sure that our words are sweet and soothing to the soul. Even in the face of adversity, our words should never pierce those for whom they are intentioned.

In our daily walk with Christ, we should pattern our thoughts to be like those offered by the Apostle Paul in his letter to the Philippians. He states,

> "Whatsoever is true, whatsoever things are honest, whatsoever things are just, whatsoever things are pure, whatsoever things are lovely, whatsoever things are of good report; if there be any virtue, and if there be any praise, think (or speak) on these things" (Philippians 4:8)

Accordingly so, it should be our mission that no one else fall victim to the negative effects of misplaced words at the mouths of the body of Christ. Our positive thoughts should, at all times; be echoed in our words.

It is my prayer for you today Brothers and Sisters that the words of your mouths be soothing to the ears of those around you. I pray that you will make it a habit to build up others as you speak positively into their lives. I pray that as you pour into others today that you will also reap that which you sow in having your spirit restored by the Father. It is my prayer that your words may be pleasing unto Him at all times so that you will be the beneficiary of His never ending grace. Finally, I pray that your deep love for Christ will be evidenced in the way you share your Christian love with those around you. I pray this prayer believing now that it has been answered in none other than the matchless name of our Lord and Savior, Jesus Christ. To God be all glory, and honor, and praise, Alleluia!

Quick Trips

1 Thessalonians 5:11	Ephesians 4:29
1 Corinthians 14:26	Romans 15:1-3, 5
Romans 14:91	Corinthians 10:23-24
2 Corinthians 12:19	

Knowing this, that the trying of your faith worketh patience. But let patience have her perfect work, that ye may be perfect and entire, wanting nothing.

(James 1:3-4, KJV)

Wait For It...

Wednesday, December 17, 2008 was a particularly difficult day for me to get through. In as much as I tried to carry on as if it were business as usual, the expression written all over my face must have surely spelled: I D-O-N-T W-A-N-T T-O B-E H-E-R-E! Try as I might, to concentrate on the task at hand, my preoccupation was such that even though my body was physically on the job, my mind was totally somewhere else. Sigh after sigh, I brooded, fretted, and then brooded some more, until finally; in true four year old form I whined to my Father in prayer about the inequality of the world and the injustice of it all.

Two praise reports received the night before had been the reason for my bad attitude, and although I was sincerely happy for those who had been blessed, the mere thought of them receiving the desires of their hearts before I did severely sank the gauge on my *faith-o-meter*. For what I thought were obvious reasons, I had made way for the spirit of envy to get a grip on me. A staunch believer in Psalm 37:4, I had placed the Lord on a timetable for when I thought my blessings should have been manifested. When they did not according to my timeline my friends' blessings only compounded my frustrations.

However, in prayer that evening, the Lord reminded me of two things. First, "For My thoughts are not your thoughts, nor are your ways My ways," (Isaiah 58:5) and "But do not let this one fact escape your notice, beloved, that with the Lord one day is like a thousand years, and a thousand years like one day." (2 Peter 3:8) I was also led to Proverbs 28:20 in admonishment which states, "A faithful man will abound with blessings, but he who makes haste to be rich will not go unpunished." Consequently, I was immediately convicted in my spirit and I repented of my jealousy and general discontent. I also asked God's forgiveness for trying to control Him.

As stated in the Tenth Commandment covetousness is a sin.

> "You shall not covet your neighbor's house; you shall not covet your neighbor's wife or his male servant or his female servant or his ox or his donkey or anything that belongs to your neighbor," (Exodus 20:17, NASB)

God would not have us take stock of our blessings based upon someone else's. Rather, and written in Habakkuk 2:3; He would have us to write down the vision and wait for its manifestation according to His perfect will and portion for our lives. As such my

Brothers and Sisters, it would behoove you to learn from my error repenting of any covetousness you may bear lest this sin take root in your spirit and be counted against you.

It is my prayer for each of you today that you will repent of any seeds of envy that may have taken root in your spirit. I also pray God's mercy and supernatural patience upon you as you wait for your due season according to His will and purpose for your life. Lastly, it is also my prayer that during your wait you will never turn your back on the Lord in the haste of your expectations. I pray this prayer believing now that it has been answered in none other than the matchless name of our Lord and Savior, Jesus Christ. To God be all glory, and honor, and praise, Alleluia!

Quick Trips

James 1:2-4	Deuteronomy 31:6
Isaiah 40:31	Isaiah 64:4
Isaiah 41:10	Isaiah 26:3-4
John 14:1-3	Hebrews 10:35-38

John 15:5

Chapter Eight:

Brotherly Love

O DEATH, WHERE IS YOUR VICTORY? O DEATH, WHERE IS YOUR STING?"

(1 Corinthians 15:55, NASB)

For Lisa

Of all the possible ways to learn of the death of a friend is via a social internet site. Yesterday afternoon presented me with said experience.

As I recounted the many memories I had of her, i.e. phone calls, conversations, laughter, and choir rehearsals; I was rendered speechless. She was gone forever. Struck with grief and saddened by the loss of life as well as the thought of her daughter being left alone, I questioned the Lord as to why He would choose to take her now. Despite my grief however, I could not cry.

Almost as if the Lord was preparing me for the tragic news earlier in the afternoon; my son felt led to share with me a word of wisdom. As we discussed the many ways the Lord had been good to us the conversation shifted to submitting one's self to the Lord even unto death. Almost instantly, Dominic explained that although he would miss me in death, the tears he would cry would be those of joy. "I am certain Mommy that you are going to heaven." Struck with awe at the maturity with which he spoke, as well as with the conviction he had for my eternal dwelling; I was blessed that the work the Lord had started within me was apparent even upon my children. (Mark 6:4)

Later that same afternoon, I would be bombarded with the death of a friend, a friend and mother who loved the Lord like myself and strived to live a life that was pleasing unto Him; a mother who left behind a daughter to mourn her loss - a daughter who, pretty much like my children; saw the wonderful work the Lord had begun.

As I sat in my dimly lit living room yesterday evening filled with sadness of the loss, I smiled with the knowledge that – though gone from us – Lisa is now in heaven. Thank you Jesus!

It is my prayer this Monday afternoon that my Brothers and Sisters in Christ join me in agreement as we lift up the family of Lisa Hutchinson. I pray that the Lord will send His comfort to them in their time of bereavement as they mourn the loss of a loving mother, sister, aunt, and friend. It is my prayer that though they may question Lisa's untimely death they will see fit to cleave to the Lord, drawing from His strength during this their time of weakness. I pray this prayer believing now that it has been answered in none other than the matchless name of our Lord and Savior, Jesus Christ. To God be all glory, and honor, and praise, Alleluia!

Quick Trips

Psalm 18:2   Psalm 55:22
Lamentations 3:31-33   2 Corinthians 1:5

Notes

Iron sharpens iron, so one man sharpens another.
(Proverbs 27:17, NASB)

Friendships in Christ

Growing up, I often struggled with the task of fitting in. Even though I was included in many circles of friends, it was not unusual for me to have been placed on the outskirts of the group as they plundered my friendship in exchange for menial tasks. On any given day, the tasks ranged from gopher to messenger, lookout to muse; or worse, the butt subject of their jokes. In exchange for their friendships, I acquiesced to their demands.

As I matured however and became wise to their game, the revelation was met with disdain and brutal defense. As time went on, I would eventually become one of them as I learned to fight fire with fire. In my own defense, I fought tooth and nail with my words in an effort to prove myself equal to those who were less than sincere in their friendship. As I gained the quip of a professional comedian, the sting of a skillful mean girl, and the droll of a sarcasm expert I ultimately evolved into that which I had loathed.

Sheer havoc was wreaked as I did to them exactly what they had done to me. As a result of the tenacity with which I divided and conquered however, my targets were soon few and far between as they chose not to endure as I had. They didn't have to. Instead of having 'friends' whose purpose in life was to abuse me, I had, in turn; become the abuser. Compounded by my regrettable harsh behavior, the loneliness now seemed even more intense than it ever had. Unfortunately, this would eventually be the mode in which I would spend most of my middle school and young teenage years.

As I moved into adulthood however, a new sense of friendship was fostered and with it the dawning of two companionships as well as one mentorship that would ultimately stand the test of time. Prevailing through marriages and divorces, pregnancies and births, job transfers and promotions, education and relocation, these relationships exist until today. Through ups and downs we comforted each other and gleaned from the other's strengths while exhorting each other through our weaknesses. Compared to the relationships of the past, these relationships were definitely from heaven.

Once I got saved however, my perception of friendships and relationships changed yet again when I found and began the most awesome and fulfilling relationship with my Lord and Savior. My Redeemer, my Confidant, and my Advocate at the inception of the relationship, He pressed into me as I to Him. As He wooed me further, He became my Provider, my Deliverer, and my Shield. As

I reciprocated His affections, He became my Cheerleader, my Support, and my Lover. Lastly as I surrendered to Him totally, He finally became the Friend whose relationship laid the groundwork for closer and more fulfilling friendships.

Incorporating His examples of patience, unconditional love, and selflessness, I now have a pattern of friendship upon which to base my relationships. Because of this training and in the shadow of His love for me, the Lord has seen fit to enrich my life with friends of His choosing who have in one way or the other added to the sweet, sweet essence of my walk with Him. As such, no longer am I questioning the motives of those around me I simply trust the God in them as I submit to His leading.

My Brothers and Sisters, with what friendships are you currently struggling? Which friends are causing you to question the costs for having them include you in their circle? Lastly, what friendships have you not submitted to the Lord or rather, have not submitted to His example of caring for and loving another?

It is my prayer for each of you today that you are able to analyze in prayer the friends and acquaintances you have chosen to include in your life. I pray that you will submit to the Holy Spirit as He shows you the persons whom He has placed in your lives as well as those who you should soon forget. Obedient to His leading, it is my prayer that you will pattern your friendships after the examples He has set in His Word so that you may ultimately be able to spiritually cultivate, sharpen, exhort, and love unconditionally those persons whom He has placed upon your path. Lastly, as you surround yourself with likeminded people of God, I pray that your collective rewards and blessings in each other may be heavenly in nature and abounding in grace. I pray this prayer believing now that it has been answered in none other than the matchless name of our Lord and Savior, Jesus Christ. To God be all glory, and honor, and praise, Alleluia!

Quick Trips

Proverbs 17:9   Proverbs 17:17
Proverbs 18:24   Proverbs 27:6
Psalm 119:63   John 15:15
1 Corinthians 15:33   James 4:4

Notes

"You did not choose Me but I chose you, and appointed you that you would go and bear fruit, and that your fruit would remain, so that whatever you ask of the Father in My name He may give to you. This I command you, that you love one another."
(John 15:16-17, NASB)

The Blessings of Brotherhood

"Good morning, Sunshine!" she sang as she entered my door this morning. It was Kelly - one of the students I taught last year - 2008. She is now a Fifth grader.

During our time together, she and I hardly ever agreed. I pushed her hard and she hated it. Swimming in marked potential she opted instead to do nothing. She had no motivation, no interest in passing on to the Fifth grade.

Unfortunately for her however, that did not stop me from trying to push her past her academic wall. The twinkle within her had already made itself known and with my prior thirteen years of experience I knew exactly what buttons to push and when. Likewise, I knew what encouragement to offer, what examples or non-examples to present.

Accordingly so, I coaxed her along whenever necessary and shared experiences of my difficulties in grade school detailing the strategies I employed to be successful. Additionally, I developed and maintained a beautiful relationship with her parents. Seldom did I show her any outward signs of frustration or worse, abandonment. In the end and although it was a difficult goal to attain, she did indeed meet the promotional requirements.

To see her now is truly a blessing! Although we butted heads then, she is now a daily fixture in my classroom each morning. When she visits, she shares all the exiting things that are happening in Fifth Grade as a result of her renewed interest in learning. To hear her tell it, she has excelled in all of her subjects this year and has been on the honor roll. With heartfelt thanks and tear filled eyes she has said that she is now in love with learning, and it is all because I did not give up on her. I am glad to have been a part of her growth for the seeds of patience, encouragement, and blessings I had planted had indeed borne fruit.

1 Peter 3:8-9 says:

> To sum up, all of you be harmonious, sympathetic, brotherly, kindhearted, and humble in spirit; not returning evil for evil or insult for insult, but giving a blessing instead; for you were called for the very purpose that you might inherit a blessing. (NASB)

Accordingly so and more than just my job, Kelly was my Christian duty. My harvest was one hundred fold. Alleluia!

My Brothers and Sisters, when was the last time you loved on someone other than those in your immediate family circle or your close and personal friends? When was the last time you returned good for evil, compliment for insult, and/or blessings for a curse?

It is my prayer for each of you today that your hand will be outstretched in search of those who need to feel the presence of the living God. I pray that you will be obedient to the leading of the Holy Spirit as you seek the Lord in earnest asking Him to direct you to those in need. Lastly it is my prayer that the words of encouragement and/or acts of kindness you minister to another will be sanctioned by the Lord and confirmed as just what was needed. I pray God's peace and blessings upon you all. I pray this prayer believing now that it has been answered in none other than the matchless name of our Lord and Savior, Jesus Christ. To God be all glory, and honor, and praise, Alleluia!

Quick Trips

Proverbs 12:14	Proverbs 18:20
Mark 4:14-20	2 Corinthians 9:9-12
Galatians 6:7-9	James 1:16-17

Not by way of eye service, as men-pleasers, but as slaves of Christ, doing the will of God from the heart. With good will render service, as to the Lord, and not to men, knowing that whatever good thing each one does, this he will receive back from the Lord, whether slave or free.
(Ephesians 6:6-8, NASB)

To the Depths of Service

The second greatest commandment of all is that we love our neighbor as ourselves (Matthew 22:37-39, NASB). But in a world in which the human race has become so self absorbed and filled with the fleeting joys of self gratification, is it any wonder why there seems to be a lack of concern for our fellow man?

Of course many would disagree with this statement by saying that their cursory attempts of holding a door open for someone, or waving their neighbor with one hand as they go out to retrieve their morning newspaper is service oriented enough. However, if we were to truly reflect upon the life of the Master, would we find our actions of service comparable to His? I think not.

As such, it is very important to remember that the Son of God came to this earth not to be served, but to serve (Mark 10:35). During His ministry, He healed the sick; comforted the downtrodden; cast out demons; delivered the lost; and spread His Father's Word. Moreover, His ultimate act of service was brought to fruition by His death on the cross as an act of forgiving our sins and redeeming us from the clutches of the enemy. Should not then His selflessness be the standard to which we daily strive to pattern? Should not our service orientation be more involved than an open door every now again or a cursory, "Hey, how are you," from time to time? Indeed, it should. As Christians we too should make it our duty to walk this earth not seeking to be served but to serve.

It is my prayer for each of you today that you will truly serve those around you. I pray that your actions, though directed at another, may be done in excellence and as if unto the Lord and all for His glory. As you minister to others, it is my prayer that your ministry will touch them at the depth of their spirits in an attempt to truly meet a need that they may possess. Lastly, it is my prayer that your spirit eyes may be made and kept open so that you will be aware of any God given opportunities to serve your fellow man that may come your way. I pray this prayer believing now that it has been answered in none other than the matchless name of our Lord and Savior, Jesus Christ. To God be all glory, and honor, and praise, Alleluia!

Quick Trips

Joshua 24:15   Matthew 25:31-45

John 21:15-18   Romans 12:1

Galatians 5:13   Galatians 6:2

1 Corinthians 10:24

Notes

Chapter Nine: Receiving, Releasing, And Perpetuating the Blessing

Blessed be the God and Father of our Lord Jesus Christ, who has blessed us with every spiritual blessing in the heavenly places in Christ
(Ephesians 1:3, NKJV)

Blessings Abound!

    Some time ago, one of my errands was to run to the post office to get some boxes for the purpose of mailing some bird seed to my mother (The price for the same bag of seed on the mainland is almost tripled at home.) When I arrived at the post office, there were only a handful of boxes left so I grabbed them all. As I did, it seemed that I did not have enough. As such, it was my intention to request some more. However, in that instant; I was led by the Holy Spirit to leave the place without requesting the extra boxes. I was obedient.

    Later that night, and again at the behest of the Holy Spirit, I began to pack the boxes. As I packed box after box, I realized that indeed there was no need for the extras. The boxes that were left were enough to meet my need. In His infinite wisdom the Lord had seen to it that I would have exactly what I needed, when I needed it. He had supernaturally provided just the exact amount of boxes I necessary to complete the task.

As is more the rule than the exception, when people talk about receiving blessings, it is usually indicative of their desire for monetary or material gain. By the world's standards, big ticket items i.e. investments, property, cars, vacations, homes, etc; are usually the means used for assessing whether a person has been blessed or not. Evidenced throughout the Bible there are indeed many references that allude to blessings of a financial nature. However, the Lord has also seen fit to provide blessings in other areas/aspects of our lives.

Evidenced in Isaiah 26:3, Psalm 136, Philippians 4:7, Psalm 30:5, Hebrews 10:30, Psalm 32:7, Leviticus 26:13, Jeremiah 33:6, Galatians 3:13-14, Psalm 5:12, and Romans 15:4 the Lord has provided us with blessings of His presence, mercy, peace, joy, vindication, deliverance, healing, redemption, favor, and time/endurance respectively. Despite the fact that these blessings are not considered to be the things some would opt for which to stand in line; they are beneficial to the body of believers, nonetheless. My Brothers and Sisters, have you accepted and acknowledged your blessings today?

It is my prayer for you today that you may be relieved of society's purview of blessings as being only monetary. I pray that you will be able to reflect upon the many gifts the Lord has bestowed upon you with an open heart. As you do, I pray that you will lift up your voice in acknowledgement and praise for the many areas of your life in which he has kept, covered, and/or secured you. I pray that you will bless His name for both the big as well as the little things. Lastly, it is my prayer that He will make His countenance to shine upon you so that others may know that you are His. I pray this prayer believing now that it has been answered in none other than the matchless name of our Lord and Savior, Jesus Christ. To God be all glory, and honor, and praise, Alleluia!

Quick Trips

Proverbs 10:6	Proverbs 28:20
Psalm 3:8	Psalm 5:12
Psalm 21:6	Galatians 3:14
Ephesians 1:3	Hebrews 6:7

Revelation 5:12

Notes

_____

_____

_____

_____

Behold, children are a gift of the LORD, the fruit of the womb is a reward.
Like arrows in the hand of a warrior,
So are the children of one's youth.
How blessed is the man whose quiver is full of them;
They will not be ashamed when they speak with their enemies in the gate.
(Psalm 127:3-5, NASB)

Newton's Third Law of Motion states, "For every action, there is an equal and opposite reaction." Imagine then if you will, a still pond in which someone has just thrown a pebble. What happens? Continuing until the initial shock has been absorbed by the depths of the water, ripples pan out from the area of the disturbance.

Transfer now that same effect upon our own lives – the decisions that we make consequently affecting our children. In reflection, what ripples are you now suffering based upon the deposit made by generations before you? Subsequently, what ripples will your children suffer based upon the deposit you are making now?

Defined by the Cambridge online dictionary as, "something that is a part of your history or which stays from an earlier time," legacy is the essence of which biblical blessings and/or curses are based. Evidenced in Exodus 20 5:6 God instructs,

> "You shall not worship them or serve them; for I, the LORD your God, am a jealous God, visiting the iniquity of the fathers on the children, on the third and the fourth generations of those who hate Me, but showing loving kindness to thousands, to those who love Me and keep My commandments." (NASB)

Accordingly so, God has issued parameters within which reward or judgment is passed down through generations based upon the acts of the generation at hand - "curses to the third and fourth generations" but, blessings and loving kindness to a thousand.

As parents, Proverbs 22:6 tells us that it is our job to,

> "Train up a child in the way he should go, so even when he is old he will not depart from it."

Thus, by teaching our children to first love God while obeying His commandments as well as to love and honor us we are the vehicle through which they will grow and blossom. At the same time, it is also our responsibility to live a life that is holy and pleasing unto Him so that no judgment is made against us thus causing said ripple effect to impact our children and their children to come.

As a result, we should not be in the habit of telling our children, "Do as I say and not as I do." Quite the contrary, for as my father says, "An example set is an example learned." If then, it is our responsibility to make the way free and clear for our children, would it not make sense that we,

> "Keep His statutes and His commandments which He has given us today, that it may go well with you and with your children after you, and that you may live long on the land which the LORD your God is giving you for all time."? (Deuteronomy 4:40, NASB)

Conclusively so, it is the wish of the Father that we pattern ourselves upon the example He has set in II Corinthians 12:14 where He says,

> "Here for this third time I am ready to come to you, and I will not be a burden to you; for I do not seek what is yours, but you; for children are not responsible to save up for their parents, but parents for their children." (NASB)

Did He not so much as love us that way first in an effort to set a precedent in the way we too should love our children?

From this day forward, we should make it a habit not only to act in a way similar to our instruction, but we should strive daily to live a life that glorifies the Father. It is in this obedience and covenant that we will enact blessings and rewards for generations to come. In conclusion, I ask you: "What legacy do you plan to leave behind for your children? Theirs? A thousand generations to come?

It is my prayer for each of you today that the lives you lead be acceptable unto the Lord and Savior Jesus Christ. I pray that you will take the call of raising the next generation in the body of Christ seriously – not as if your life depended on it, but as if the lives of your children and their future generations did. I pray that in covering your children with His word as well as with holy examples of Christian living they will be able to experience the love of our Savior. I also pray that the result of your steadfast obedience to Him will be to usher in the blessing of Abraham your children so rightfully deserve. Finally, I pray God's peace and protection over you as the task of raising and mentoring children in any capacity is an impossible task without God's infinite grace, mercy, and guidance. I pray this prayer believing now that it has been answered in none other than the matchless name of our Lord and Savior, Jesus Christ. To God be all glory, and honor, and praise, Alleluia!

| Ephesians 6:4 | Colossians 3:21 |
| Proverbs 13:24 | Proverbs 29:14 |

Proverbs 19:18   Proverbs 29:17
Psalm 115:14-15   Proverbs 20:7

Notes

> But let all who take refuge in You be glad;
> let them ever sing for joy.
> Spread your protection over them
> that those who love your name may rejoice in you. (Psalm 5:11, NASB)

Smooth Transition of Leadership

Just this month (January 2009), our school made a transition of leadership from a principal who had effectively served the school for the past five years to someone whom we had never met. Understandably so, this change ushered in a sense of fear and insecurity about what was to come. However due to the wisdom and eloquence employed by the impending principal during her transition period, as well as the concerted prayer of a team of intercessors, not much of a hiccup was felt by the staff. As a matter of fact, it was business as usual. Although on a much smaller scale than what is expected tomorrow, this scenario lends itself as an example of how both the power of intercessory prayer, wisdom, and the grace in which one operates can help to smooth even the most worrisome situations.

In like fashion today, Tuesday, January 21st, 2009; will begin an unprecedented new era in the history of our country; the United States of America. The end result of a very long and arduous journey by both President elect Barack Obama and Vice-President elect Joe Biden, the process has been marred by many a heated debate, malicious slander, and vehement criticism. Despite its history however, this day will nonetheless prove to be the realization of the combined hopes and dreams of many an African American, as well as the fruition of a vision held by generations of others gone before us. While still for others, it will prove to be the bane of their very existence. Nevertheless, no matter the emotions experienced, tomorrow will symbolize the day we will all embark on a journey together that will ultimately reveal the true nature of the nation, the undeniable heart of its people.

No matter our personal views however, as Christians it is our duty to come together in prayer to uplift not only our leaders, but also our nation during this time of transition. Moreover, as our newly elected leaders try to recharge our nations failing economy, it should likewise be prudent to pray the blessing of Deuteronomy 28:10-11 upon our nation. Lastly, as we step into uncharted waters, it should be our united prayer that our nation as a whole return to the ways of God, upon which it was founded so that the

Lord will see fit to breathe new life and restoration upon us all, ultimately healing lands.

My prayer for you today is simply that you will first put aside your personal agendas so that you would allow the Spirit to lead as we all lift up our country in prayer and supplication to the most High God. Let us all pray that our nation will turn from its wicked ways and seek God's face so that He might heal our land. I pray this prayer believing now that it has been answered in none other than the matchless name of our Lord and Savior, Jesus Christ. To God be all glory, and honor, and praise, Alleluia!

Quick Trips

2 Chronicles 7:14	Titus 1:1-7
1 Timothy 5:17	1 Peter 5:3
Matthew 18:1-4	1 Timothy 2:1-4
James 5:16	

Notes

Then teach them the statutes and the laws, and make known to them the way in which they are to walk and the work they are to do.
(Exodus 18:20, NASB)

Teachable Moments

When my children and I feel like enjoying a silly evening together, we opt to do so in front of the TV watching reruns of SpongeBob. Although riddled with elementary comedy, childish idioms, and ridiculous puns the show is a fertile ground for discussions on Christian living and principles. As we watch, we are able to analyze the various characters to classify their behavior as either Christian or non-Christian.

One such example of this is Mr. Krabbs' egregious love of money. Often risking the lives of his friends and employees, and the happiness of his daughter Pearl, Mr. Krabbs will stop at nothing to amass money and treasures - definitely, not Christian. Another example would be the many ways in which Spongebob Squarepants thinks nothing of bending over backwards to serve not only his friends but also the customers of the Crusty Crabb – definitely Christian. Based upon these classifications, the children and I would converse for hours as we analyze the motives and inclinations of the characters. Referencing and aligning scripture verses to their specific acts, we would eventually come to a decision about the Christian validity of their ways.

What I like most about these teachable moments is that sound spiritual teaching is also infused with their TV time. By doing this, I consider myself planting the seeds of wisdom in my children from a very young age. Evidenced in Psalms 119:34, understanding of the law – the Word – lends itself to its following wholeheartedly and ungrudgingly. By immersing my children in God's Word even during their leisure times, I am ensuring that His law will be etched upon their hearts therefore giving them a solid foundation in the attainment of His Holy wisdom. This in turn will guarantee that they will never depart from the training they received in their youth. (Proverbs 22:6)

My Brothers and Sisters what opportune moments are you not utilizing to engrain God's word upon the hearts of your children? What teachable moments are you not using to minister to those children who have been entrusted to your care? Christ took advantage of teachable moments all the time. Would He not want us to pattern ourselves after Him to share the good news of the Gospel?

It is my prayer for each of you today that you will be susceptible to the teachable moments that arise in your lives. As you grow your children up in the ways of the Lord, I pray God's wisdom on your endeavor. I pray that He will impart the gift of wisdom upon you so that you may gain supernatural insight into His Word for the direct purpose of edifying the lives of your children now so that they will not desire to depart from His ways later. I pray this prayer believing now that it has been answered in none other than the matchless name of our Lord and Savior, Jesus Christ. To God be all glory, and honor, and praise, Alleluia!

Quick Trips

Genesis 18:19	Matthew 19:4
Deuteronomy 6:6-8	Deuteronomy 29:29
Psalm 34:11	Psalm 32:8
Proverbs 4:1-11	Proverbs 5:1
Proverbs 8:32	Proverbs 13:22

Notes

The unfolding of Your words gives light;
It gives understanding to the simple.
(Psalm 119:130)

This Little Light of Mine

One of my most memorable moments of children's church was singing the song, "This little Light of Mine." My favorite part was when everyone would chime in on key, "Hide it under a bushel? No! I'm gonna let it shine." However, even more fulfilling than that was when our teachers would prompt us to sign the song in unison. What a treat! Twenty or more children would play peek-a-boo with their make-believe baskets vowing never to hide their Jesus light.

What I did not know then however, was that the song was based on scripture. Found in Matthew 5:14-15 the Apostle states,

> "You are the light of the world. A city set on a hill cannot be hidden; nor does anyone light a lamp and put it under a basket, but on the lamp stand, and it gives light to all who are in the house.

"Hide it under a bushel? No!" Accordingly so, think for a moment if you will about how moths are attracted to a lit bulb in the dark, or for that matter, of yourself in a dark room with only a candle to light the way. What happens? Does not the light draw and keep your attention? Yes, it does.

You see, the nature of light is to captivate and draw people/things closer to it. Should that not be the task of all Christians in the world – to tell others of Jesus and draw them closer to Him? How then can we captivate others with the Light who dwells within us? What actions can we take that would exemplify the love of Jesus to those around us? As Christians, "a city set on a hill," should be symbolic of how bright our lights should shine. If, as the song states, it would be difficult to, "hide our lights under a bushel", imagine then how much more complex it would be to hide the lights of a city set on a hill. Accordingly so my Brothers and Sisters I ask you today, "How bright is your Jesus light?" Is it set high on a hill for all to see His glory manifested in and through you, or have you chosen to, "Hide it under a bushel?"

It is my prayer for each you today that the Light that dwells within you may never be diminished. I pray that through your thoughts, words, and actions your light will not only captivate, but draw others onto our Lord. Lastly, I pray that God will reveal His will for making your light shine brighter for all to see. I pray this prayer believing now that it has been answered in none other than the matchless name of our Lord and Savior, Jesus Christ. To God be all glory, and honor, and praise, Alleluia!

Quick Trips

John 12:36	Proverbs 13:9
Isaiah 42:16	Isaiah 49:6
Ecclesiastes 11:7	Matthew 6:22-23
Luke 11:33-36	Ephesians 5:8-10
John 1:9	John 12:46
John 3:19-21	John 8:12

Notes

> I love those who love me;
> and those who diligently seek me will find me.
> (Proverbs 8:17 NASB)

Wrestling with a Purpose

One memory I have of an ex-boyfriend was the fervor with which he enjoyed wrestling. No, not the high school formatted Olympic styled wrestling as one would guess, but rather the scripted, choreographed, Hollywood sanctioned likeness of the same. His love for the sport was so strong that it caused him - no matter where he was or what he was doing – to abruptly drop everything on Monday and Thursday evenings to take in the shows at home.

In true sportsman like commentary he would narrate blow after blow as I sat there in utter amazement at the sheer cluelessness of his efforts to draw me in. Incited at my unmitigated gall to dare ask of him, "Why on the earth are you sharing this with me?" a heated discussion of his weekly vice about its reality or lack thereof would always ensue. Despite the many debates we held however, his ardent enjoyment waned not as he vowed never to forsake his passion for the sport. And, up until the time our relationship ended - six years from its inception; he never did.

Although I look back now in hindsight and laugh at those many encounters I often think back in admiration of the distinguished passion and high esteem in which he cleaved to the sport. Because of his refusal to give up his hobby he was blessed, so to speak, with the qualities fellow fans would find endearing. For example, he was much better equipped for discussing the topic amongst friends and he thoroughly understood the game's statistics. What is more, throughout the years he has been able to maintain a deeper appreciation for the sport and all that it entails.

Though a worldly representation, this same passion of refusing to let go can be found in the Bible. Evidenced in Genesis 32:24 – 29 Jacob, brother of Esau; wrestled with God refusing to let go until He was blessed. A difficult struggle complete with collateral damage as well as deliberate personal injury, Jacob wrestled with God while cleaving to His promises until God saw fit to bless him. Can you imagine the sheer audacity Jacob must have had to have endured a fight with God even through to the end result of a limp? Whether gall or desperation, Jacob's passion was such that he simply did not plan to take no for an answer nor did he chose to have wasted his efforts to simply give up.

Would God not have us all wrestle with Him in this manner as well? In seeking God to keep His promises and by living a life that is pleasing unto Him in both worship and in following His commandments, can we too not cleave to Him so passionately and determinately that He has no other choice than to bless us according to our portion? It has always been my opinion that the Lord seeks to uphold every single promise He has made to us however, and most often than not; we are the ones who defeat this purpose and stand in the way of our own blessings. In closing consider this: One cannot play a game of hide and go seek with another who refuses to look. Are you actively seeking to establish a personal relationship with Christ? With whom or what are you wrestling?

My Brothers and Sisters what is it that you would seek to wrestle God for in accordance to the promises He has made to you? What actions are you not completing or stance are you not assuming that in the end does not relay your desperation and boldness to the Lord?

It is my prayer for each of you today that you would diligently seek to wrestle with the Lord in fulfillment of His promises. I pray that though you may be wounded in the battle that you will be bold enough in Him not to let go until you are finally blessed. I pray a blessing of endurance upon you all so that though you may be tempted to release your grip, you will not fall prey to the guises of the enemy. Lastly, I pray that you will strive daily to push into the Holiest of Holies where our God abides so that you may be richly blessed according to your desires for and faith in Him. I pray this prayer believing now that it has been answered in none other than the matchless name of our Lord and Savior, Jesus Christ. To God be all glory, and honor, and praise, Alleluia!

Quick Trips

Matthew 6:33	Matthew 6:8
1 John 5:14-15	Luke 11:9-10
John 14:12-14	Philippians 4:19
Philippians 4:6-7	3 John 2

Notes

Now unto him that is able to keep you from falling, and to present you faultless before the presence of his glory with exceeding joy, to the only wise God our Savior, be glory and majesty, dominion and power, both now and ever. Alleluia!

(Jude 24-25, NASB)

About the Author

A modern day Jonah, Danielle M. Walcott ran from God's purpose for her life - writing. After several attempts to write lyrics, publish and perform secular poetry, as well as edit other's writings Danielle finally came to the realization of her gifting - to pen the characteristics of God's heart. As a result, she finally surrendered her pen to the move and voice of God in the fall of 2008. Accordingly so, Danielle has shared her gift of insight through the sentiments expressed in her first published daily devotional.

An educator by trade, Danielle enjoys speaking publicly as well as creating curriculum for the advancement of the Ancient Paths - God's ways of old. Mother to a pair of sixteen year old twins, Dominic and Dominique, Danielle maintains a life filled with service to her fellow man; life-long learning; and an active social life with family and friends.

A recent transplant to the mainland, she currently calls Atlanta, Georgia her home. However the island of St. Croix in the United States, Virgin Islands is where her heart remains to this day.

Made in the USA
Charleston, SC
13 February 2014